EFFECTIVE
FOUNDATION
MANAGEMENT

EFFECTIVE FOUNDATION MANAGEMENT

14 Challenges of Philanthropic Leadership— And How to Outfox Them

Joel J. Orosz

ALTAMIRA
PRESS

A Division of
Rowman & Littlefield Publishers, Inc.
Lanham • New York • Toronto • Plymouth, UK

AltaMira Press
A division of Rowman & Littlefield Publishers, Inc.
A wholly owned subsidiary of The Rowman & Littlefield Publishing Group, Inc.
4501 Forbes Boulevard, Suite 200
Lanham, MD 20706
www.altamirapress.com

Estover Road
Plymouth PL6 7PY
United Kingdom

British Library Cataloguing in Publication Information Available

Library of Congress Cataloging-in-Publication Data

Orosz, Joel J.
  Effective foundation management : 14 challenges of philanthropic leadership—
and how to outfox them / Joel J. Orosz.
      p. cm.
  Includes bibliographical references and index.
  ISBN-13: 978-0-7591-0986-5 (cloth : alk. paper)
  ISBN-10: 0-7591-0986-9 (cloth : alk. paper)
  ISBN-13: 978-0-7591-0987-2 (pbk. : alk. paper)
  ISBN-10: 0-7591-0987-7 (pbk. : alk. paper)
  1. Charities—Management. 2. Endowments—Management. 3. Nonprofit
organizations—Management. I. Title.

  HV41.O758 2007
  361.7'632068—dc22   2007015745

Printed in the United States of America

♾™ The paper used in this publication meets the minimum requirements of
American National Standard for Information Sciences—Permanence of Paper for
Printed Library Materials, ANSI/NISO Z39.48-1992.

For Dr. Russell G. Mawby and
Dr. Norman A. Brown,
Chairman Emeritus and
President Emeritus, respectively,
of the W. K. Kellogg Foundation:
wise mentors and good friends.

CONTENTS

PART II   THE SEVEN DILEMMAS OF MANAGING FOUNDATIONS

FOREWORD

"**A**lways remember that the grantseeker comes to you, psychologically, on his knees." The speaker was Waldemar A. Nielsen, Rhodes Scholar, accomplished program officer, celebrated author, and raconteur nonpareil, and I was a rapt audience of one. The time was 1992; the occasion was a seminar on Mid-Continent Philanthropy that Wally had organized, and the place was the Aspen Institute's Colorado headquarters. Nielsen told me that, as a young program officer at the Ford Foundation, he had heard that sentence from the renowned Abraham Flexner (1866–1959), author of the famed Flexner Report on Medical Education in the United States, produced while he was a program officer at the Carnegie Foundation for the Advancement of Teaching, and later a motive force behind John D. Rockefeller Sr.'s General Education Board, the disease-bashing, segregation-fighting, prototype of the Rockefeller Foundation. It was an extraordinary moment: the field's iconic program officer had shared this lesson with the field's foremost critic, who had then passed it along to me. I felt privileged, indeed, to be the latest link in this oral chain that transmitted the hard-won wisdom of grantmaking to future generations of practitioners.

Along with the sense of privilege, however, came more fuel for the simmering frustration I had experienced since entering the philanthropy field eight years before. Although it was great to learn this lesson about grantseekers in 1992, it would have been far better if I had learned it in 1986, when I was just starting out. Now that I knew it, I could share it with others, but as a program officer at the W. K. Kellogg Foundation, what chances, realistically, would I have to teach it to other program officers in other foundations, in other parts of the nation? Most of all, why wasn't this insight from one of the giants in the foundation field captured in a book that could be shared with other program officers, especially new ones entering the field?

When I first donned the grantmaker's mantle, I was by training a historian, and by vocation, a museum curator. I was used to learning about a new field first from the academic lessons taught through its heritage and then through the educational programs devised by its professionals, programs that could lead to certification or accreditation in that field's work. It came as a surprise to me to learn that, although the foundation field had a long and illustrious history, few people working in philanthropy knew anything about it, and worse, few cared to learn its lessons. It was even more shocking to learn that there was only a patchwork of educational opportunities available, none of which led to any kind of certification, and that nothing remotely resembling the rigorous American Association of Museums' accreditation program existed in the foundation world. In fact, there was not even a good book to read that introduced the newcomer to the craft of grantmaking or to the mysteries of foundation management.

The foundation field, for all of its money, prestige, and influence, was not a profession, but rather an agglomeration of generalists, immigrants from other fields all, who now toiled—some with distinction, some with confusion—in this strange and wonderful world of philanthropy. I learned my craft as a grantmaker, thankfully, from wise and generous mentors: Russ Mawby and Norm Brown, to both of whom this book is gratefully dedicated, and especially the late Peter R. Ellis, whose patient coaching will always be remembered with gratitude. But ultimately, even with all of their help, I had to learn by doing, by "experimenting upon humans": the Kellogg Foundation's applicants and grantees. I believe that I served most of them well, but I still wince when I recall some, especially during my early days in the field, who were innocent victims of my "beginner's errors."

As the years passed, and as my experience and confidence grew, I still marveled that the two basic texts I had sought in vain in 1986—the book on the craft of grantmaking and the book on the mysteries of foundation management—still remained unwritten. With the aid of a professional study leave from the Kellogg Foundation in 1999, I was able to fill the first gap by writing *The Insider's Guide to Grantmaking*, a comprehensive introduction to the skills needed to become an effective foundation grantmaker. I was advised, however, to forget about writing the second book, for reasons that, I must admit, have some merit (although obviously not enough to prevent me from accepting the challenge).

It was clear to me, and to all others with whom I shared my ideas, that it would be impossible to write a useful book about the management of foundations without dealing frankly with the flaws and dysfunctions into which the leaders of foundations, both executive officers and board members, often fall. And it was just as clear to some of my advisors that, by writing about such problems, I would only be handing ammunition to the enemies of organized philanthropy, who would use it in order to mount assaults on foundation freedom and possibly even upon the existence of foundations as a legal entity.

I wish I could say that these fears are groundless, but there is no doubt that this book contains enough information about, and examples of, foundations behaving badly (or just plain foolishly) to provide aid and comfort to any vindictive critic of the foundation world. More than once I have wondered if I might be braiding the rope that will be used by foundation lynch parties.

My convictions eventually won out, however, over my fears. I simply understand no other way for a field to improve than to expose its bad practices, promote its good ones, and strive always to replace the former with the latter. And it is hard to understand how new foundation CEOs and board members are going to learn their craft without absorbing lessons—both good and bad—from the heritage of the field, without learning where pitfalls lurk and without absorbing the basics of sound practice.

Moreover, I do not believe that foundations have many true enemies who will deliberately misuse the facts and arguments presented in this book. To be sure, there are a number of hard-hitting critics—Joel Fleishman, Peter Frumkin, Leslie Lenkowsky, Kathleen McCarthy, Peter Dobkin Hall, Rick Cohen, Stanley Katz, Susan Raymond, and David Hammack come immediately to mind—who have taken foundations "to the woodshed" for past transgressions and who may use information presented in this book as an occasion to do so again. All of these scholars, however, are thoughtful seekers of the truth, and their criticisms, painful though they may be, are well founded and well worth considering. Even the bluntest critic of foundations over the past generation, Pablo Eisenberg, is a man of high integrity whose attacks on foundations are based on his honest convictions, not on malice. Nor do I foresee extensive political fallout, for the leaders of the Senate Finance Committee, which has taken the lead in overseeing foundations, Senator Max Baucus (Democrat-Montana) and Senator Charles Grassley (Republican-Iowa), have pursued a regulatory regime that can be characterized as tough but fair. They want to reform foundations, not destroy them.

Those who objected to an airing of the foundation world's dirty laundry, however, are not paranoid (and even if they were, we must remember that paranoids do have some *real* enemies). There are a small number of ideologues, both on the far left and the far right of the political spectrum, who would like nothing better than to use the information found in this book to the detriment of foundations—the far left–wingers because they believe that foundations do not do enough to redistribute wealth, the far right–wingers because they believe that foundations do too much to redistribute wealth. It is my conviction, however, that their political agendas will be so transparent that the vast majority of reasonable people will reject out of hand their self-interested misuse of information gleaned from this book.

Ultimately, I concluded that the process of hiding the foundation world's flaws from a small splinter group of ideologues has also hidden valuable lessons we must learn from each other, and also, ironically enough, concealed methods of fixing those flaws. We need to trust the good sense and the good judgment of the scholars, lawmakers, and members of the general public, who will be able to discern the difference between (to paraphrase Lyndon Johnson) chicken salad and chicken droppings. In any case, more than a century of silence has done little to improve practice. It is time to give shared voices and open dialogue a chance.

I hope that this volume will take its place alongside *The Insider's Guide* as a handbook for new leaders in philanthropy, a place to learn the wisdom of the past and the good practice of the present, as a prelude to creating the positive social impact of the future. This is a vision that is so compelling, it is worth risking criticism to achieve, and it is in this spirit that I commend these chapters to you: may you make good use of them in order to make the most of your noble calling of improving the lives of people.

Joel J. Orosz, PhD
Kalamazoo, Michigan
March 14, 2007

ACKNOWLEDGMENTS

This book had its genesis seven years ago, when I was writing my first volume on philanthropy, *The Insider's Guide to Grant-making: How Foundations Find, Fund, and Manage Effective Programs*. This was essentially a how-to manual for program officers new to philanthropy, but some reviewers then—and several readers since—suggested that its audience would benefit from a better understanding of how foundations are managed. This was clearly beyond the scope of *The Insider's Guide*, but it suggested that a companion volume exploring the most common traps of managing foundations (and how to avoid them) might be in order. Taken together, *The Insider's Guide* would serve as the program officer's day-to-day instruction manual, while the companion volume would explain the broader context of foundation management under which program officers operate.

The first opportunity to explore ideas for the new book came as a result of an invitation to be one of the lecturers in the Waldemar A. Nielsen Issues in Philanthropy Seminar Series held at Georgetown University from October of 2001 to April of 2003. This series was funded by the Ewing Marion Kauffman

Foundation and named in honor of "Wally" Nielsen (1917–2005), the former Ford Foundation program officer who had become celebrated for two books of hard-hitting (and constructively critical) analysis of the philanthropic field, *The Big Foundations* (1972) and *The Golden Donors* (1985). It was an honor to accept the invitation, all the more so because I had enjoyed the privilege of being Wally's program officer when he sought—and received—a grant from the W. K. Kellogg Foundation in the mid-1990s.

I owe a debt of gratitude to Dr. Virginia Hodgkinson, research professor at the Georgetown Public Policy Institute of Georgetown University, who invited me to present one of the nineteen Nielsen lectures, on October 18, 2002, under the title of "Terra Incognita: The Poorly-Understood Challenges and Trade-offs of Foundation Management." This lecture was well received, and it essentially served as the outline for the book that is in your hands.

I want to thank two successive CEOs of my employer, the Dorothy A. Johnson Center for Philanthropy and Nonprofit Leadership of Grand Valley State University, Dr. Donna VanIwaarden and Dr. Kathy Agard, for their unfailing support of my research and writing on this project. A number of Johnson Center employees helped in ways too numerous to mention but too valuable to leave unnoticed: Angela Vander Hulst, Allison Lugo Sáenz, and Cristin Heinbeck.

I express my gratitude, as well, to Dorothy A. Johnson herself, who in her long tenure as a trustee of the W. K. Kellogg Foundation has been an exemplar of foundation governance done well. Other W. K. Kellogg Foundation colleagues whose wisdom always provided a beacon for me include Dr. Robert Long, Chris Kwak, Tom Reis, Alandra Washington, and especially the late Dr. Peter R. Ellis, teacher extraordinaire.

I appreciate, as well, the wise counsel of the faculty of the Grantmaking School: Lynn Alvarez, Hugh Burroughs, G. Albert Ruesga, and Gabriel Works, as well as its new (as I write these words) director, Dr. Kenneth L. Gladish.

My family—wife Florence and children Caroline, Anita, Marianna, and Andrew—deserve a medal for their forbearance, especially when work on this book occupied time normally reserved for evening, weekend, and vacation recreation.

My editors at Rowman & Littlefield, Serena Krombach and Claire Rojstaczer, deserve every kudo imaginable for their unflagging support, unending good humor, and constructive suggestions for improvement. Other Rowman & Littlefield employees who have earned my thanks, in this case for their marketing chops, are Meagan Smith, Molly Ahearn, and Lita Orner.

Sandy LeRoy, the proprietor of Executive Format in Kalamazoo, Michigan, went above and beyond her duties of transcribing the manuscript—her sharp eye for consistency and wise suggestions for changes materially improved the quality of this book.

Finally, my appreciation to the anonymous readers who reviewed the book in manuscript form and shared many helpful ideas for changes. All of them were instrumental in catching errors, identifying ambiguities, and providing fresh ideas. This book has been much improved by their exertions; any flaws that remain I will cheerfully accept, in paraphrase of the words of Shakespeare's Prospero: "These things of darkness I acknowledge mine."

INTRODUCTION

FOUNDATIONS AND FAILURE

Foundations fail. Not invariably, of course, nor always egregiously, but far too often. If the Gospel according to St. Luke is correct—if of those to whom much is given, much is expected—then foundations, which are given so much in the way of resources and the freedom to deploy them, are not delivering expected results. Jed Emerson, Senior Fellow with the Generation Foundation, says of foundations, "They are both essential and they are missing in action."[1] Professor Michael Porter of the Harvard Business School puts it as bluntly as possible: "Foundation scandals tend to be about pay and perks, but the real scandal is how much money is pissed away on activities that have no impact. Billions are wasted on ineffective philanthropy."[2] This is not entirely the fault of foundation leaders, for the simple-sounding act of giving away money to good causes is fraught with unexpectedly knotty complexities. This is hardly a novel insight; back in 1967, Warren Weaver, a longtime vice president of the Rockefeller Foundation, wrote that "giving away money wisely is an extraordinarily subtle and difficult task, with moral, social and intellectual complications that keep the conscience active and the mind bothered."[3]

The lion's share of the blame for poor performance, however, can be laid at the leadership's door, for the failures of foundations do not issue from irrational factors or mysterious forces, but rather from predictable challenges and recognizable dilemmas. A hard-won knowledge base exists—garnered from the painful failures and creative successes of past foundation initiatives—that offers ways to meet the challenges and resolve the dilemmas, but most new foundation leaders are unaware of its existence, or worse, ignore its lessons entirely. This book introduces the new foundation CEO, vice president, board member, chief programming officer, program director, or program officer to seven challenges and seven dilemmas of foundation leadership and management, along with some strategies for meeting and resolving them. Mastering the "formidable fourteen" challenges and dilemmas of foundation management is not a guarantee of foundation success, but ignoring them is virtually a guarantee of continued foundation failure.

FOUNDATION HISTORY AND ACHIEVEMENTS

Foundations have had plenty of time and experience to grapple with the formidable fourteen. The first modern grantmaking charitable foundation in the United States, the Peabody Education Fund, commenced operations in 1867. The pioneering multipurpose foundations arrived early in the twentieth century, with the establishment of the Carnegie Corporation of New York in 1911 and the Rockefeller Foundation in 1913. After World War II, foundation formation accelerated rapidly, on its way to the more than 80,000 such institutions in operation in the United States today. Michael Porter is correct that these organizations make many ineffective grants, but they also notch significant successes. Foundations have supported programs that eliminated hookworm and yellow fever in the United States, wiped out smallpox worldwide, developed the polio vaccine, pioneered effective treatments for HIV/AIDS, and are today working toward the global elimination of polio, tuberculosis, and HIV. As impressive as this roll call of achievements is, it is limited to health care; in other fields as diverse as talking books for the blind, a uniform color for school buses, the rocketry research of Robert Goddard, and the establishment of 911 emergency operator systems, foundation funding has provided the margin of success. Leaders of foundations such as these have bequeathed to us methods to overcome the challenges and resolve the dilemmas of foundation management.

Why, then, has it proved so difficult for so many foundation leaders to tap into that knowledge base? The experience of two of the greatest entrepreneurs in U.S. history provides an insight. John D. Rockefeller created the largest monopolistic corporation in the history of the United States. W. K. Kellogg transformed the breakfast tables of the Western world. Yet both of these legendary entrepreneurs agreed that it was much easier to create and operate the enterprises that produced their great fortunes than to manage the grantmaking foundations that their business success made possible. How could such a thing be? We all know how difficult it is to create wealth, so how could it be tougher to be an effective grantmaker?

A closer look, however, reveals some very good reasons why Rockefeller and Kellogg were correct in their analysis. Profit-making companies have been with us for centuries, while by contrast, as we have seen, it was not until after World War II that foundations began to appear in any substantial numbers. We have similarly had much longer to study the workings of business than the workings of philanthropy, for the first schools of business administration made their appearance late in the nineteenth century, while the first academic centers to study philanthropy did not appear until the last quarter of the twentieth century. Businesses of any size are usually managed by MBAs, while foundations, even the largest of them, are almost invariably managed by people who were trained for some other kind of work entirely.

Moreover, foundation CEOs usually are not chosen because of extensive experience in the field of philanthropy. Donors creating new foundations typically choose people they know and trust to be CEOs, which usually means their attorney, or their certified public accountant, or the retired president of the family business. Long-established foundation boards are apt to select foundation CEOs from the ranks of those who have distinguished themselves in high-profile managerial roles: those of university president or newspaper publisher seem particularly attractive. And, one after another, these new foundation CEOs discover a surprising fact, namely that managing foundations (no matter how extensive or impressive their previous managerial experience), is devilishly difficult. Belatedly, they learn that Rockefeller and Kellogg were right.

INHERENT DIFFICULTIES OF FOUNDATION MANAGEMENT

To be fair, some of the difficulty inherent in managing foundations is simply beyond the control of any foundation leader. No one would dream of placing at the helm of a major corporation, or in the chair of its board of directors, someone who had no experience whatsoever in that firm's business; yet, such appointments are routine in the foundation world, even among its largest and most sophisticated members. Much foundation failure, therefore, arises from "rookie mistakes": simple inexperience. Beyond this problem, however, lie forces that arise from the highly distinctive—some would say just plain weird— realities of the foundation world.

First, no foundation leader can help the fact that foundations alone among the millions of corporate entities in the United States have no clear customers or constituency. Commercial organizations must answer Peter Drucker's second question—Who is our customer?—or they quickly go out of business.[4] Politicians know their constituents, or they lose the next election. But who, exactly, are a foundation's customers? Are they the nonprofit grantees? Are they the clients whom these grantees serve? Are they the people of a city, state, or nation? Customers and constituents are powerful; they can turn to other providers or other politicians if the service they receive is not satisfactory. Nonprofits and the clients they serve are much less powerful; they depend upon foundations for support, and it is much harder for them to walk away from poor service. This confusion about who the customer is, and the lack of incentives to provide good service to the customer, makes it difficult for foundation leaders to focus on a clear course of action.

A second difficulty that foundation leaders can do little about is the lack of a reliable yardstick with which to measure success or failure in their field. Foundation leaders who previously worked in other sectors are used to reliable yardsticks: the businessperson to the balance sheet, the politician to the pollster, the nonprofit manager to fund-raising results. When the numbers from these yardsticks are positive, they know they are succeeding. A foundation's endowment, however, performs independent of its grantmaking effectiveness; the foundation's grantmaking can be lousy this year, and the foundation will nonetheless get more money with which to do an even lousier job next year. Nor are the results of the grantmaking clear, for the outcomes of grants are expensive to measure, difficult to attribute to your own foundation, and usually take many years to manifest themselves. Did this year's grantmaking result in society-changing impact, or was it a complete waste of time and money? Foundation leaders have only a dim inkling, and it will be years before the actual results emerge, if they ever do. It is enough to make a leader pine for the harsh discipline of the marketplace or the rough justice of the polling place.

The third difficulty that bedevils foundation leaders arises from the peculiar nature of power in the foundation world. CEOs from other spheres—from the commercial or government sectors—are used to giving orders to subordinates and expecting their orders to be obeyed. Once transported to the foundation boardroom or executive chair, however, such leaders encounter an alien power dynamic. Although it is true that the "golden rule"—those who have the gold make the rules—does apply, foundation leaders soon discover that their rules are not necessarily obeyed. Foundations initially have lots of leverage over grantseekers, but once the grant is made, their leaders discover that much of that leverage evaporates. Grantees cite realities on the ground as reasons to interpret grant agreements quite liberally, and sometimes to flout them altogether. Foundation leaders have to learn new skills of leadership that are distributive rather than concentrated, that rely on persuasion rather than compulsion. This distributive style has its strengths, but the authority to execute a strategy quickly and efficiently is not among them. Simply put, having a largely independent delivery system makes it much harder for foundation leaders to deliver good results.

The final, and perhaps most vexing, difficulty that perplexes foundation leaders is the simple fact that there is no profession of grantmaking. Leadership of professionalized organizations is made easier by the fact that such organizations are largely self-defining and self-policing. They subscribe to a codified set of good practices, and professionals are expected to operate within these prescribed boundaries. If they stray, a governing body can (and will) apply sanctions to the misbehaving organization or individual. Organizations upholding the high standards of the profession earn the respect of the general public. Foundation leaders have none of these valuable tools at their disposal. There is no set of codified good practices, no governing body to sanction misbehaving organizations or individuals, and consequently little sense of shared responsibility for behavioral standards. Foundation philanthropy does not do nearly enough to agree on standards of good practice, nor to raise the bar of its own performance. The result, sadly, is that new practitioners make the same mistakes their predecessors made before them, and they become better grantmakers not by deliberate plan but rather by trial and error. It brings to mind Dorothy Parker's wry observation: "It's not one damned thing after another. It's the same damned thing over and over." It is extremely difficult, therefore, for foundation leaders to demand professionalism from the foundation's employees when just what "professional" means in the foundation context has never been defined by the field.

So foundations, with their inherent lack of clear understanding of their business, their inherent inability to measure results, their inherent inability to control their delivery system, and their inherent lack of a strong tradition of professionalism, are consequently inherently difficult to manage. These difficulties are daunting for any manager, for they are built into the system and not amenable to any leader's control.

THE "FORMIDABLE FOURTEEN" CHALLENGES AND DILEMMAS OF FOUNDATION MANAGEMENT

Moreover, the formidable fourteen challenges and dilemmas also stand in the way of successful outcomes and positive impacts. Fortunately, there are responses to these fourteen that *are* within the control of foundation leaders, and yet those leaders too often ignore them. And when these challenges and dilemmas are ignored, foundations flounder and fail. Paying attention to the formidable fourteen will not make foundations automatically easier to manage, but confronting them will make it easier for leaders to guide foundations to more successful outcomes.

These fourteen can be divided evenly into two categories. The first consists of seven vexing challenges that arise from the highly idiosyncratic nature of the foundation field. Because these problems are so distinctive to the field, they are not readily perceived or understood in their full dimensions by leaders whose main training and experience lie outside of foundations. The second category consists of seven inescapable dilemmas or trade-offs that arise from strategic decisions made in the course of managing every foundation. Like the challenges, most of these dilemmas are characteristic to the foundation field, and they prove baffling to those whose preparation and experience occurred in other sectors. Although there are no simple answers or easy resolutions to any of the formidable fourteen, there are discerning management approaches and informed decision-making techniques that, if learned by foundation leaders, can surmount the challenges and minimize the negative consequences of the dilemmas. Learning these approaches and techniques will make the foundation far more effective and ultimately make its leadership far more successful.

That which bedeviled such incisive business minds as John D. Rockefeller and W. K. Kellogg still befuddles foundation managers and leaders today. It is no overstatement to say that it is not necessary for *every* foundation leader to master the formidable fourteen: only those who want to be *effective* need do it.

THE SEVEN CHALLENGES

The most striking thing about the seven challenges is how mundane they appear at first glance. Leaders who come to the foundation field from other professions are apt to assume that such things as preemployment training and a cohesive internal culture are as much a part of grantmaking as of their former fields. Once they discover that this is not the case, however, leaders tend to discount the importance of such things. Their failure to address these challenges comes back to haunt them, as they discover that effective operation of their foundation proves to be a maddeningly elusive goal. The seven challenges are deceptively vexing, but they are hardly imponderable, if only foundation leaders would take the time to understand how to deal with them.

1. Lack of pre- and postemployment training. Everyone associated with foundations, from the chair of the board to the program staff, has at least one thing in common: they were all trained to do something else entirely. Given the absence of expertise, how can you prevent your foundation from becoming the uninformed leading the unprepared toward the undefined?

2. Lack of a cohesive culture. Foundation staffers have been recruited from a riotous diversity of backgrounds; every field, it seems, from astronomy to zoology is represented. When a staff consists of people utterly diverse in their socialization and worldview, how can you create a team that works effectively together?

3. Lack of a salutary external discipline. Society's organizations are driven to improve by salutary external disciplines—for commercial organizations, the market; for government organizations, the next election—but foundations have no salutary external discipline. How can you prevent your foundation, in the absence of such external discipline, from becoming too comfortable and risk-averse?

4. Lack of reliable feedback. Few are brave—or foolhardy—enough to offer constructive criticism to people who have the unchecked power to deny their next request for funding. How can you seek and use unvarnished feedback from applicants and grantees?

5. Lack of an accepted body of good practices. In most fields, practitioners have agreed upon a set of procedures that lead to good outcomes, and they attempt to place them into everyday practice. In the absence of agreed-upon standards of practice, how can you prevent your foundation from becoming like Garrison Keillor's Lake Wobegon, where every program officer is "above average"?

6. Lack of ideological cohesion between board and staff. Foundation boards tend to be drawn from the conservative world of their founders, while staffs tend to be drawn from the progressive world of social activists. How can you prevent your foundation from splitting into an acrimonious "red state/blue state" division?

7. Lack of ideological cohesion within the staff. Foundation staffs tend to divide into the "bleeding heart" subculture of the program staff, the "bean counter" subculture of the finance staff, and the "bureaucrat" subculture of the administrative staff. In the absence of a unifying principle such as the profit motive, how can you prevent your foundation from suffering the fate of the former Yugoslavia?

THE SEVEN DILEMMAS

If the seven challenges appear mundane at first glance, the seven dilemmas are often subtle enough that they are missed altogether, even when the trade-offs they inevitably engender are hobbling a foundation's performance. Leaders who regard low overhead and highly strategic operations as unalloyed positives, for instance, seem incapable of understanding that, in the foundation context, such operating styles invariably usher in rigidities that hamper a foundation's ability to be nimble and seize ephemeral opportunities. Ironically, every blessing in foundations has a curse at its core, and although the curse can never be eliminated entirely, its effects can be mitigated if the nature of the trade-off is appreciated and addressed.

1. Low overhead versus high overhead. A low overhead operation maximizes the grantmaking budget, but it simultaneously minimizes the value that foundations can add to grantmaking through technical assistance, due diligence, evaluation, and dissemination. How can you resolve the dilemma so that the foundation's operating style creates the greatest good for the greatest number?
2. Strategic planning versus flexibility. Strategic planning focuses the foundation's resources on targets of high value to society, but the very act of focusing reduces the foundation's flexibility to seize unforeseen opportunities or respond to unexpected crises. How can you resolve the dilemma so that you can concentrate your resources without unduly freezing your flexibility?
3. Broad versus deep. Foundations are torn between the urge to be the philanthropic equivalent of a wide-spectrum antibiotic, solving a wide range of human problems, and a designer drug, focusing narrowly on a single big problem. Too often, they try to be both and end up more like a patent medicine, fruitlessly promising cures for all social ills. How can you resolve the dilemma so that your foundation takes on no more—and no less—than it is capable of handling?
4. Innovation versus implementation. Foundation leaders see great value in making investments in new, untried, and promising ideas so that better answers might be found to problems that vex humanity. Foundation leaders, however, also see great value in making investments in established organizations, to help them become more effective in delivering services to improve the lives of people. How can you reconcile the conflicting claims of innovation and

implementation, or is there a way to effectively support both at the same time?

5. Expert based versus community based. What could be more sensible than designing programs based on the advice of the people who have intensely studied the problems? On the other hand, what could be more sensible than designing programs based on the advice of people who will have to live with the outcomes? How can you craft programs so that the often contradictory claims of experience and data can be reconciled?

6. High uncertainty versus low uncertainty. Every foundation leader dreams of high-risk triumphs, but all realize that while many foundation leaders have been fired for failing, none has ever been cashiered for mediocre success. How can you set a course that allows your foundation to take on an appropriate level of risk in its programming?

7. High profile versus low profile. Every foundation leader dreams of his or her foundation being featured prominently in *The Chronicle of Philanthropy*, but it is every foundation leader's nightmare to have that paper criticize the foundation. How can you resolve the dilemma so that your foundation's profile is high but not bearing a bull's-eye?

To understand the seven dilemmas, foundations must remember the wisdom of G. W. F. Hegel, who argued that tragedy is not the collision of right and wrong but rather the collision of right and right. It is right to operate with low overhead, to maximize grantmaking. It is also right to operate with high overhead, to maximize the value that foundations can add to their grantmaking. To choose one over the other is absolutely the right thing to do; and simultaneously, it is absolutely the wrong thing to do. And this holds true, as well, for the other six dilemmas, for there is no such thing as a silver bullet choice that yields only cost-free good outcomes. Hegel was correct: when two rights collide, the outcome is tragedy. Effective foundation management, therefore, is the art of balancing these in-escapable trade-offs so that the tragedy is minimized and the foundation's potential for success is maximized.

The formidable fourteen are the rocks upon which many a foundation leader has seen his or her boat founder. It is not, however, preordained to end this way. Many a foundation leader in the past has steered his or her ship clear of these fourteen rocks and in the process has found a way through the shoals and shallows. The "charts" they bequeathed to us will not work for all foundations, or under all circumstances, but for most foundations, under most circumstances, they provide a way of keeping the ship afloat. They deserve consideration in detail.

HOW TO READ THIS BOOK

This book was written for anyone whose *privilege* it is to provide leadership to a grantmaking foundation—on the executive side, CEOs, vice presidents, chief programming officers, program directors, and program officers; on the governance side, board members. This book can be attacked in two different ways. The reader can either approach the seven challenges and the seven dilemmas in a systematic, cover-to-cover fashion, or he or she can skip around, focusing on the challenge or dilemma that is most pressing to him or her at the moment. There is utility in either method, but more value in reading through systematically. Concepts introduced in the early chapters of the challenges recur throughout the rest of the book, and a deeper understanding will follow if the chapters are read in order.

The challenges and dilemmas will be explained—and ideas for effectively managing each will be offered—using a "mixed methods" approach. Examples of success stories and horror stories, guidelines to follow, helpful tips, diagnostic questions, time-tested rules to follow, pertinent data, and experiential anecdotes will all be employed as appropriate to demonstrate how foundation leaders can meet the challenges and manage the dilemmas for maximum effectiveness.

The author of this book is well aware that there is far more art than science in the management of foundations. A certain level of failure is not only likely when one is responsible for the stewardship of charitable resources, but also downright inevitable. This book is not, therefore, a passport to perfection. Although I cannot promise flawless performance to those who read this book, I can—and do—promise that mastering the responses to the challenges and dilemmas will make you a better foundation leader and your foundation a more effective operation, with greater positive societal impact.

NOTES

1. Jed Emerson, "Foundations: Essential and Missing in Action," *Alliance Online Extra*, March 2006, www.allavida.org/alliance/axmar06b.html?pnd (10 March 2006): 8.

2. Matthew Bishop, "The Business of Giving," *The Economist* 378, no. 8466 (February 25–March 3, 2006): 4.

3. Warren Weaver, *U.S. Philanthropic Foundations: Their History, Structure, Management, and Record* (New York: Harper & Row, 1967), 109–10.

4. Peter E. Drucker, *The Practice of Management* (New York: Harper and Row, 1954), 54–56.

I

THE SEVEN CHALLENGES OF
MANAGING FOUNDATIONS

CHALLENGE 1: LACK OF PRE–
AND POSTEMPLOYMENT TRAINING

THE GREAT FOUNDATION TRAINING GAP

Imagine, if you will, that you are in court facing a serious felony charge. You turn to your lawyer and ask, "So, where did you attend law school?" Your attorney replies, "Never went to law school." Concerned, you ask, "But you did pass the bar exam, right?" Back comes the answer, "Nope, I never took the bar exam." Nearing panic, you ask, "But, you do have extensive litigation experience, don't you?" Your lawyer responds, "Naw, up until last week, I was a taxidermist."

This, sad to say, is analogous to the scenario that too many grantseekers face with their foundation program officers. The analogy, of course, is exaggerated: Grantseekers will not do hard time if their program officer fails them. A good deal of precious foundation funding is at stake, however (more than $40 billion in grants as of 2006), so the mind boggles that foundation leaders have been generally satisfied with the paucity of preemployment training and the meagerness of postemployment training opportunities for their staffs.[1] When pressed on the matter, foundation leaders say that their employees' wide variety of backgrounds prevents foundations from falling into "groupthink" and confers a sort of "hybrid vigor" upon the field. There can be no doubt that there is some merit to these justifications. The question is, however, whether these benefits are greatly outweighed by the harm that unprepared and untrained program officers visit upon applicant and grantee alike.

Ask anyone who has dealt with foundations about this question, and—provided your conversation is strictly off the record—you will hear a long litany of complaints about the caliber of the program officers with whom they must deal. Applicants and grantees complain of arrogant attitudes and ponderous practices, including unnecessary steps, demands for superfluous documentation, and outright misinformation. They become particularly annoyed when discussing the ill-conceived requests for proposals (RFPs) emanating from foundations, offering funds for projects that neither nonprofits, nor the people they serve, need or want.

One longtime (and long-suffering) grantseeker tells of an encounter with an untrained grantmaker: "First he asked for hundreds of pages of documents: our IRS 990 tax return, our audited financial statement, our strategic plan and our accreditation report. Then he made us rewrite the proposal three times. Then he spent a whole day visiting us. Finally, nine months after we started with him, he abruptly denied our request because it didn't fit the foundation's grantmaking guidelines—something he should have figured out during our first conversation with him."[2] Another program officer recently approached me for an explanation of "what was wrong" with the nonprofits that had failed to respond to his foundation's latest RFP, apparently never dreaming that the fault may lie with the quality or the relevance of the RFP itself!

Suffer as they will, applicants and grantees have little choice but to suffer in silence. Few of them are eager to criticize the practices of program officers possessing the sovereign power to arbitrarily turn down their next grant request. Regulators of the foundation field, particularly staffers of congressional oversight committees, do not suffer from the same reticence, and they have increasingly sounded alarms about transgressions committed by foundation personnel unfamiliar with even the most basic laws and regulations governing their field.

Untrained program officers present the most visible problems, but the "training gap" challenge flows all the way up the organizational ladder to the very top. A well-publicized series of investigative reports conducted by the *Boston Globe* in 2003–2004 revealed foundations in which the salaries paid to top officers exceeded their charitable payouts, and others in which private jets were used to transport board members to routine meetings in faraway exotic locales on the foundations' dime. More often than not, such peccadilloes reflected ignorance rather than avarice. When a trustee of one small (assets of $5 million) private foundation was asked to explain his single-year salary increase from an already astronomical $1 million to $1.5 million, his response was a classic of cluelessness: "I had to marry off a daughter and it took a little bit more than I had anticipated."[3]

WHY TRAINING AND EXPERIENCE ARE NOT VALUED IN THE FOUNDATION FIELD

How did things come to such a sorry pass? The answer lies in the long and slow development of the foundation field. In the late nineteenth century, the large numbers of commercial entities made it financially feasible for universities to offer programs of business administration, and that credential rapidly demonstrated its value in practice. Similarly, in the early twentieth century, the growth of government at all levels encouraged the development and acceptance of university programs of public administration. Foundations, by contrast, were few in number and mostly small in size during the first century of their development. The potential market was too small for universities to create programs of foundation administration, so no credential was ever developed for the foundation field. In the absence of such a credential, no standard of professionalism ever emerged. Foundations became, consequently, one of the last bastions of the enlightened generalist, or less charitably put, the rank amateur.

The ranks of these generalists/amateurs have been growing in recent years, albeit still at a measured pace. It surprises many, even those who make their living in the field, to learn that a vast majority of foundations are small in size and bereft of paid staff. Of those foundations that do employ staff, a great majority (more than 76 percent) work for the relative handful of the largest foundations (those that boast $100 million or more in assets).[4]

One might reasonably assume that, if preemployment preparation for these employees is scarce, foundations would at least insist upon postemployment training. Surprisingly few, however, do so. The Ford Foundation and the California Endowment are among the handful that makes serious postemployment training in grantmaking a priority. Most foundations provide little more than a bare-bones orientation to their new hires, and many a program officer will tell you that his "training" consisted entirely of being ushered to his desk, being handed a stack of proposals, and receiving a hearty admonishment to "make good grants."

Given the rarity of both pre- and postemployment training, a judicious observer might assume that foundations would at least consider prior experience in philanthropy to be a prerequisite for every position, especially that of chief executive officer. In fact, this is not true. When establishing new foundations, donors tend to hire CEOs based not on experience in the field but rather upon the basis of personal trust or loyalty. Nearly always, their choice is their attorney, or their accountant, or the retired CEO of their commercial firm; worse, much worse, they sometimes choose fraternity brothers, relatives, or best friends. Larger foundations tend to be less idiosyncratic in their CEO choices but no more respectful of foundation experience. Board members almost invariably turn to leaders who have distinguished themselves in other fields—higher education, commercial enterprises, government service—to take the helm of their major foundations.

All of this is more than a little curious. In most fields, training and experience are highly valued. If you need surgery, for example, you would undoubtedly prefer that a trained surgeon, rather than a university president, conduct the operation. You would also prefer that the surgeon have many years of operating room experience, rather than none at all. Foundation board members rationalize their choices by claiming that many years of successful grantseeking qualifies a university president, for example, to lead a grantmaking organization. This justification, however, is very much like choosing a longtime patient as chief of surgery on the rationale that someone who has endured a number of successful operations must be fully qualified to supervise surgeons. Moreover, untrained and unprepared CEOs typically lack enthusiasm for training their program officers, perhaps because the idea of having subordinates who know more about philanthropy than they do is a bit unsettling to them. The typical unready CEO, therefore, is highly unlikely to become a champion of field improvement through education.

Foundation leaders, unsurprisingly, have tended to make a virtue of nonprofessionalism. They speak eloquently of the necessity of hiring the great thinkers and the foremost practitioners in fields of programming interest to serve as program officers and even as CEOs. It is far better, they say, to have people in place who have demonstrated expertise in health or youth development, for example, than someone who has specialized knowledge about the processes of grantmaking, especially since such "mere technical skills" can be absorbed through on-the-job training. The "mere technical skills" needed by program officers to do their jobs effectively, however, cover an enormously wide range. At minimum, program officers must have a strong understanding of nonprofit organizations, including the essentials of

organizational development and life cycles, and generally accepted accounting principles. They must be familiar with the
body of law and regulatory rulings that structure the daily operation of both nonprofit organizations and foundations. They
must have a comfortable working knowledge of evaluation theory and practice, ranging from due diligence techniques before
a grant is funded to longitudinal studies after the grant-
supported project has been closed. And they need to be skilled
in the art of managing funded programs for which they do not
possess the usual managerial power to hire and fire employees.
Clearly the vast range and the great depth of these skills require
more than just individual on-the-job training.

In defiance of this logic, however, there are a number of foundation leaders who go still further, paraphrasing Alexander Pope,
to suggest that in grantmaking, "a little learning's a dangerous
thing." This line of thought compares program officers to bread,
which turns stale, then moldy, if it exceeds its ideal shelf life. Program officers who stay too long become arrogant and lose touch
with the realities in the field; therefore the foundation's policy
must be to rotate their program officers every five years or so.
(Indeed, this "five years and out" approach was the policy of the
Ford Foundation for several decades.) In short, according to this
way of thinking, not only is training nonessential, but significant
experience and training is actually a *bad* thing. Interestingly,
though, the dangers of experience seem to affect only program
officers; these foundation CEOs and board members rarely seem
to apply the five-year rule to their own positions!

Foundation CEOs and board members, however, do apply
one thing equally to program officers and their own positions:
their general disdain for education. To be fair, until very recently, there have been few opportunities for a foundation's top
leadership to learn about the idiosyncrasies of foundation management and governance that render service in this sphere utterly distinct from superficially similar leadership posts in other
sectors—even different from leadership roles in other nonprofit

sector organizations. CEOs and board members alike must learn to come to terms with the inherent realities of the foundation world discussed in the introduction—the fact that most foundations have no clear customers or constituencies; that they have no reliable yardstick for measuring success or failure; that managerial power in the foundation world is distributed rather than concentrated; and that there are no professional standards for grantmaking. And these are only the overarching difficulties; the fourteen challenges and dilemmas explained in the rest of this book must also be learned and mastered. Even the most self-confident CEO or board member must concede that these are skills worth learning.

It is also the case that training, whether for program officers or foundation executives, becomes a harder sell over time. Foundation employees tend to don a mantle of expertise the moment they take their jobs. To admit that they have gaps in their preparation is tantamount to admitting to applicants and grantees alike that "the emperor has no clothes." The tendency of foundation employees, therefore, is to protect their credibility by hiding under that mantle, and the longer they hide under it, the less likely they are to emerge from it. As a result, there are many seasoned program officers, vice presidents, and CEOs working in foundations who have a trove of experience, and even considerable expertise in foundation work, who suffer— and more importantly, make applicants and grantees suffer— from their lack of basic training in the history, techniques, legal framework, and ethics of philanthropy.

TWO WAYS TO BRIDGE THE GAP: BEFORE AND AFTER

If this training gap was merely an abstraction, it would be of no great moment. Unfortunately, it is very tangible. Unprepared and untrained foundation employees make life miserable for nonprofit leaders and, more to the point, squander resources earmarked for the people whom these nonprofit organizations serve. This gap is the root cause of Michael Porter's observation that "billions are wasted on ineffective philanthropy."[5] Just as you can't hit what you can't see, you can't effectively practice what you don't fully understand. The training gap is like an insidious, self-imposed tax upon foundations, reducing the good they can do and diminishing their positive impacts on society. That's the bad news. The good news is that this tax is undeniably self-imposed, which means it can easily be self-removed.

There are two ways to bridge the training gap: the "before" and the "after." The "before" method seeks to hire staff already prepared to do the foundation work, while the "after" method seeks to hire people who can be trained after being employed. As a practical matter, the "before" method is hard to achieve, for the philanthropic market is relatively small—fewer than 19,000 people were employed by U.S. foundations in 2006, and that includes finance and other nonprogramming professionals—and universities, until very recently, have not established pertinent academic programs.[6] The Center on Philanthropy at Indiana University has pioneered both a master's and a PhD degree in philanthropy.[7] These degrees are not vocational; they do not teach aspiring foundation professionals specific techniques of effective grantmaking. They do, however, offer an intensive grounding in the theory, philosophy, history, and ethics of philanthropy, thus providing an invaluable intellectual basis on which to base work in charitable foundations. As these degrees prove to be successful and popular, no doubt other universities will follow in Indiana's footsteps and establish other "before" academic programs.

As valuable as a master's or doctorate in philanthropy might ultimately prove to a foundation leader, earning such a degree at Indiana in the expectation of being hired by a foundation currently represents the triumph of hope over reality. Foundation leaders do not as yet highly value a theoretical preparation for work as either a program officer or a CEO. A much more practical form of the "before" employment training, therefore, is to concentrate on the nonprofit organizations that form the delivery system of foundations. Here, since the potential market—employment in America's 1.9 million nonprofit organizations—is so much larger than that of employment in foundations, there are many more educational choices.[8] More than forty institutions of higher education offer advanced degrees in nonprofit topics, ranging from a master's of nonprofit organizations degree at Case Western Reserve University to degrees that combine two or more disciplines, such as the master's of public administration with a nonprofit concentration at Grand Valley State University.[9]

Although these nonprofit studies programs do not pretend to train their students specifically for foundation work, because nonprofits are the delivery system for foundations, the lessons they teach about nonprofit management do impart a valuable knowledge base for foundation leaders. And if nonprofit studies graduates do perchance become foundation leaders after having led nonprofit organizations, they will be better prepared to handle the challenges and trade-offs for having worked for many years as grantees of foundations.

As previously noted, the scarcity of "before" training has not made foundation leaders advocates of "after" training. In the vast majority of foundations, everyone from beginning program officer to CEO to board chair gets little more than a basic orientation before taking up their daunting responsibilities, and many get no preparation at all. One explanation for this is simply a lack of "after" supply. Although both the Forum of Regional Associations of Grantmakers (the umbrella organization for the nation's thirty regional associations of grantmakers) and the Association of Small Foundations offer a diverse menu of foundation training programs—governance for trustees, management and leadership for CEOs, introduction to grantmaking for program officers—none have the on-staff expertise needed to go beyond the basics, nor the capacity to train all of the newcomers to the foundation field.[10] Moreover, all are membership organizations, not educational institutions, so training tends to be a sideline to their main work of field-building and public policy activity.

A handful of foundations have distinguished themselves by creating in-house training capacity and requiring new employees to avail themselves of it. The Ford Foundation has one of the oldest and most comprehensive training programs in the field, and all Ford program officers, both domestic and international, are required to complete it. The California Endowment instituted a training program early in its existence, and its program officers as a result are among the best prepared in the field. Other foundations, while not creating in-house training, have availed themselves regularly of external opportunities for educating their employees; among these are the Bill and Melinda Gates Foundation, the Ruth Mott Foundation, the Missouri Foundation for Health, the Rockefeller Brothers Fund, the W. K. Kellogg Foundation, and the Endowment for Health in New Hampshire.

Beginning in 2001, the Ford Foundation began sharing its in-house training materials with other foundations under the banner of the GrantCraft project, which offers case studies, videos, and curricular materials, all at a reasonable price.[11] GrantCraft staff also present seminars based on their materials at grantmakers' annual meetings.

The first university-based program for teaching techniques of advanced grantmaking to foundation program officers is The Grantmaking School, a program of the Dorothy A. Johnson Center for Philanthropy and Nonprofit Leadership of Grand Valley State University in Grand Rapids, Michigan.[12] I founded The Grantmaking School in 2004, with the assistance of a major grant from the W. K. Kellogg Foundation. Its faculty consists of former program officers from such foundations as Kellogg, the California Endowment, and the C. S. Mott and Packard Foundations, and it offers intensive three- to five-day seminars in locations around the nation. Current courses (with others in development) are Advanced Proposal Analysis and Advanced

Portfolio Management. It should be noted that the New York School of Philanthropy, which was affiliated with Columbia University as early as 1904, does not take the "earliest" crown from the Grantmaking School, for it actually trained social workers, not foundation program officers, and eventually evolved into Columbia's School of Social Work.[13]

Other universities have joined the Grantmaking School in the foundation training arena, including Stanford, Indiana, New York University, and the University of Missouri at Kansas City. These pioneering programs are providing proof of the concept that there is a demand among foundation employees for training in the art and craft of grantmaking and foundation management. As they establish the market, other universities will surely follow with new programs.

THE TRAINING GAP: THE BEGINNING OF THE END?

The pioneering programs have made some encouraging inroads on the training gap and have already solved the seemingly paradoxical low-cost problem. For years, entry-level training programs offered by the Council on Foundations (since transferred to the Forum of Regional Associations of Grantmakers) and the Association of Small Foundations, along with assorted regional associations for grantmakers, have been subsidized by private foundations on the theory that training was not highly valued, and charging the full cost would chase away potential customers. The pioneering university-based programs have charged full retail prices, and program officers—supported by their foundations— have readily paid the tariffs. The reason is that the training programs, even the most expensive, are actually cheap in relation to a foundation's grantmaking. The $1,950 charged by the Grantmaking School for a three-day Advanced Proposal Analysis course, for example, is equivalent to one very small grant, even by a foundation with only modest assets. A poorly trained program officer will waste much more money than this on every grant made. Hence, the training, properly understood, is a tremendous bargain.

These pathbreaking educators offer a beginning, but only a beginning. Even collectively, they lack the capacity as of yet to meet the demand for advanced training in the field. It is particularly important that educational programs for trustees and CEOs be expanded, not only because it is intrinsically good to have trained foundation leaders but also because trained leadership is more likely to understand the need for, and allocate funds for, the training of program officers. The field has made strides in this direction; until 1999, no educational programs existed outside of trade associations, and there was not even a book that introduced program officers to basic good practices in grantmaking. Less than a decade later, all of the programs mentioned are up and running, and two solid books, *The Insider's Guide to Grantmaking* and *Grantmaking Basics*, are in print.[14]

Much more needs to be done, however, to overcome the challenge posed by the training gap. Until very recently, foundations have truly represented the uninformed leading the unprepared toward the undefined. Society deserves better. There must be not just more education providers and more training but also the rise of a culture of learning in foundations large and small nationwide. "As this process proceeds," observed former Ford Foundation program officer and longtime foundation world critic Waldemar Nielsen, "ignorant, amateurish and petty philanthropy, which still characterizes a good part of the activity of even the very large foundations, should become an early casualty."[15] Universities need to work with thoughtful practitioners to create a knowledge base about foundation philanthropy, and from that, to generate principles of good practice. Then, these principles need to be taught to foundation leaders and program and program officers, both new and veteran, so that the field becomes characterized not by well-meaning but poorly prepared amateurs but rather by well-prepared and effective professionals. It is a goal that is eminently achievable, in a reasonable time frame, and at a comparatively modest cost. If it is achieved, society will get much more "bang" for every foundation buck expended.

"We know so much more now than ten years ago," says Jed Emerson, "and the reason we do is because certain organizations —foundations included—have experimented and learned. . . . The stakes are too high not to build on these initial steps."[16] Emerson is correct that simply applying the emerging knowledge base will improve foundation effectiveness and hence social impact. With the stakes so high, and the risks so low, how could any foundation leader be reluctant to take the simple steps required to close the training gap?

NOTES

1. Loren Renz, Steven Lawrence, and Josefina Attenzai, *Foundation Growth and Giving Estimates* (New York: Foundation Center, 2006), 1.

2. Interview with a nonprofit leader who requested anonymity, 11 September 2006.

3. Beth Henley, Francie Latour, Sacha Pfeiffer, and Michael Rezendes, "Some Officers of Charities Steer Assets to Selves," *Boston Globe*, 9 October 2003.

4. www.foundationcenter.org/findfunders/statistics/gm_staff.html (5 March 2007).

5. Matthew Bishop, "The Business of Giving," *The Economist* 378, no. 8466 (February 25–March 3, 2006): 4.

6. www.foundationcenter.org/findfunders/statistics/gm_staff.html (5 March 2007).

7. www.philanthropy-iupui.edu/exmu.html (12 September 2006); www.philanthropy.iupui.edu/phd.html (12 September 2006).

8. Independent Sector, "Facts and Figures about Charitable Organizations" (Washington, D.C., Independent Sector, 2006), 1.

9. www.case.edu/mandelcenter (12 September 2006); www.gvsu .edu/jcp (12 September 2006).

10. www.givingforum.org and www.smallfoundations.org (12 September 2006).

11. www.grantcraft.org (12 September 2006).

12. www.grantmakingschool.org (12 September 2006).

13. "New York School of Philanthropy," Wikipedia, en.wikipedia .org/wiki/New_York_School_of_Philanthropy (5 March 2007).

14. Joel J. Orosz, *The Insider's Guide to Grantmaking: How Foundations Find, Fund and Manage Effective Programs* (San Francisco: Jossey-Bass, 2000); Barbara D. Kibbe, Fred Setterburg, and Colburn S. Wilbur, *Grantmaking Basics: A Field Guide for Funders* (Washington, D.C.: Council on Foundations, 1999).

15. Waldemar A. Nielsen, *The Golden Donors: A New Anatomy of the Great Foundations* (New York: Dutton, 1985), 431.

16. Jed Emerson, "Foundations: Essential and Missing in Action," *Alliance Online Extra* March 2006, www.allavida.org/alliance/axman06b .html?pnd (10 March 2006): 8.

2

CHALLENGE 2: LACK OF A COHESIVE CULTURE

THE EFFECTS OF POLYGLOT PREPARATION

Imagine, if you will, that you have just been named the CEO of a large manufacturing firm. Your task will be difficult, but one thing will ease your burden: your entire management team will all hold MBAs from various business schools. This shared educational background provides them (and you) with a common language, a common worldview, and hence the beginning of a common culture. It does not guarantee harmony, teamwork, or success, but it does at least assure a certain level of coherent communication and a shared set of tools to do the work.

Now imagine that you have just been named the CEO of a large charitable foundation. Your employees all have disparate college majors, hold various academic degrees, worked in different sectors of the economy, and occasionally seem to have resided on other planets. For any issue under discussion, the reactions are apt to be nothing if not varied. Those who majored in the hard sciences will demand, "Where are the data?" Those who majored in the social sciences will ask, "What are the cultural and sociological contexts?" Those who majored in a technical field will ask, "What are the metrics?" Those who majored in the humanities will ask, "What is the big picture?"

Similarly, differing professional experiences spread staff reactions all over the map. People whose training and socialization were in the private sector prior to joining the foundation will demand, "What is the bottom line?" Those whose training and socialization were in the public sector will inquire, "What are the policy implications?" Those whose training and socialization were in the nonprofit sector will query, "How will this affect people?"

With all of this riotous diversity in education, training, and experience, achieving consensus among a foundation staff—indeed, just reaching an agreement on the nature of the issue at hand—can be a mind-numbingly difficult task. The staff's divergent worldviews, diverse priorities, and even different ways of perceiving and knowing make managing foundations the most challenging leadership task since that of the overseer at the Tower of Babel.

THE SCOURGE OF "FOUNDATIONESE"

In fact, the Tower of Babel is an apt metaphor because all of this diversity expresses itself within foundations most openly in their employees' language. Unsurprisingly, given all of the differences on the staff, communication is rarely a simple matter. Foundation leaders, for whatever reason, do not tend to force everyone to use a common tongue, and the Swiss example of having four official languages, while interesting, is simply too cumbersome. What has evolved at most foundations of any size, therefore, is a common jargon that transcends the motley educational and vocational backgrounds represented on the staff. Esperanto may have failed as a language in the rest of the world, but its spirit lives on in this jargon, which Dwight McDonald, in his 1956 study of the Ford Foundation, christened as "foundationese, where meaning, such as it is, drapes itself in

Latin-root polysyllables." McDonald had little affection for the tongue he had named, for he referred to it as a "contemporary dead language."[1] His judgment was not borne out by events, for in the half century that followed, foundationese has developed into a vital national dialect, one that enables a program officer from a community foundation in California to communicate with a private foundation program officer in Connecticut. Foundationese "de-babbles" internal communications and provides a basis, albeit tenuous, for a foundation to start building a common culture.

For all of its benefits, however, foundationese is undoubtedly an atrocity against the noble English tongue. It has evolved into a passive voice–plagued, catchword-clotted language that offends the ear and benumbs the brain. Program officers can, and often do, create sentences like this one: "The RFP requires an LOI be filed by the aspiring NGO specifying a client-driven, fully transparent initiative with embedded metrics that will demonstrate the impactfulness of the intervention and suggest its replicability should meta-evaluation applications indicate desired outcomes are in place at project termination." Of course, one could more economically say, "We are looking for ideas that come from the people we are trying to help and that, ultimately, will make a measurable positive difference in their lives."

If there are any lingering doubts that foundationese is running amok, the works of Tony Proscio put them quickly to rest. In *Bad Words for Good: How Foundations Garble Their Message and Lose Their Audience* and *In Other Words: A Plea for Plain Speaking in Foundations*, Proscio brilliantly dissects the vacuous pomposity of the worst elements of foundationese.[2] His books should be absolutely mandatory reading for all foundation leaders, from trustees to program officers, for all who read them will find ways to communicate more clearly.

Despite Proscio's cogent efforts, however, foundationese stubbornly marches on, partly because come the Apocalypse, the only two things left standing are likely to be cockroaches and jargon, but mostly because of the big benefit it provides: the basics, however bloviated, for a common culture. Without it, foundations slouch back toward the Tower of Babel. Is there a way, then, to create the blessings of a common culture without embracing the excesses of foundationese?

Fortunately, there is such a happy medium. The first step toward achieving it is simple in concept but difficult in execution; namely, it is to define key terms. This may seem elementary on first glance, so much so that foundations rarely bother to do it, and the result is always chaos. Take, for example, the familiar term *community*. Foundation stallers can, and often do, use that very word simultaneously, but with myriad different meanings. For example, program officer A is thinking about a geographical community; B is thinking about a community of common interests; C is thinking about a community defined by race; D is thinking about a community defined by income; E is thinking about a community defined by educational levels; and F is thinking about a community defined by age group. Unless definitions are made explicit, the six program officers in this example could speak past each other for years while ostensibly talking about the same thing.

As bad as the problem of definition can be within a foundation, it can rapidly metastasize into a disaster when program officers from different foundations come together in council. I once participated in a meeting sponsored by a key philanthropic intermediary organization in which the discourse rapidly deteriorated when the discussion turned to the concept of community-based services. To some participants, this could only mean services provided *by* those indigenous to certain neighborhoods, while others defined it as services provided *for* those residents. Some may dismiss this as a semantic fuss over words of one syllable, but these semantics very nearly derailed the entire meeting.

Foundation leaders often resist such definitional work, fearing that it will turn into persnickety pettifogging along the lines of President Clinton's infamous statement, "That depends on what the definition of 'is' is." There is no question that arriving at common definitions is hard and often tedious work, but it is essential if a foundation is to "de-babbleize" its communications. Not every word need be defined, of course, but it is necessary to specify the key concepts at the heart of the work so that a common language can develop and the basis for a common culture can be established.

Once key words and phrases are defined, the excesses of foundationese can be tackled. The problem is not the fact that there is jargon; foundations need a common language in order to create a common culture, and a foundation version of Esperanto is the easiest and cheapest way of creating that language. The problem is that foundations have allowed that Esperanto to degenerate into a putridly passive morass. Most foundationese reminds one of Truman Capote's critical judgment of Jack Kerouac's work: "That's not writing—it's typing!" Foundation leaders, therefore, should not attempt to ban foundationese because it is flabby; instead they should make it their mission to whip it into fighting trim.

A few simple changes will eliminate the worst offenses. The passive voice is the biggest problem. Program officers love to write passive sentences because they can sound authoritative without requiring actual research, such as, "It is said by some experts that the positive impacts upon the target audience of youth were accelerated by the grant made by our foundation." It is not only more accurate but also infinitely more readable to say, "Experts Smith and Jones commented about our grant's positive impact upon its youthful target audience." Wringing the passive voice out of foundationese will go far toward making it meaningful and understandable.

The mutation of nouns into verbs is another problem, and the noun *impact* is the poster child for this insidious process. Impact began its life as a noun (as in to create a positive impact), but it has mutated into a verb, as in "the misuse of language negatively impacts the reader." Impact should remain a noun, especially when there is a perfectly good verb, *affect* (as in "proper use of language positively affects the reader's understanding of the sentence"), to employ in impact's stead. Other mutated nouns-to-verbs include *tasked, missioned, incented,* and *granted.* The sheer dreadfulness of the sentence "I have been tasked to support health-missioned organizations through incented programs of granted dollars" is so self-evident that no further comment is necessary.

Finally, commonly misused buzzwords should be banished. Some words, such as *unique,* which properly means "singular, one and only one in all the world," are so badly misused as to have become utterly meaningless. When a program officer writes that her project is the "most unique" that the foundation has ever funded, she is not making a meaningful comparison, but rather is offering mindless blather. Tony Proscio offers more meaningless words to avoid: *comprehensive, linkage, learnings,* and *mechanisms.*[3] Just these three reforms—pruning the passive, eliminating mutated nouns, and barring misuse of buzzwords—would transform the foundationese beast into a beast of burden, an Esperanto that can carry a common culture upon its back.

THE PLAGUE OF DILETTANTISM

One other extremely important element must be considered in any effort to create a more effective foundation culture, that of self-identity. If you ask an engineer how she would describe herself, she would reply that she is an engineer. If you ask a nurse, he would say that he is a nurse. Ask a foundation program officer, however, and the answer is apt to be muddled. All program officers, remember, were trained in other fields. So, if a program officer was trained as a lawyer, how does she identify herself, as an attorney or as a grantmaker? It is possible, of course, that she may regard herself as both an attorney *and* a grantmaker, but most people tend to lean strongly toward their early training and experience; hence, in this example, the law usually prevails over philanthropy.

This natural tendency is strongly reinforced by those foundation leaders who are apt to view program officers as analogous to a loaf of bread, with a limited shelf life. If your leaders are urging you to return to your old field in four to five years, it hardly makes sense to stop thinking of yourself as an attorney and start regarding yourself as a grantmaker.

The consequences of this "identity crisis" upon foundation effectiveness are significant, even dire. If foundation work is but a brief interlude in a career spent mostly doing other kinds of labor, what motivation do foundation workers have to improve their craft? If foundation staff spend their time going to the conferences and reading the literature produced in their old fields, how will they find the time to attend philanthropy conferences and read the philanthropy literature? And if they do not keep up, how will they learn about the latest ideas, techniques, and approaches in philanthropy? To ask the question bluntly, are they practicing professionals in philanthropy, or are they dabbling dilettantes?

The sad truth is that many program officers never think of themselves as grantmakers, never see themselves as connected in any meaningful way to the field of philanthropy, and always envision a day not far in the future when they will leave the foundation field. They are reinforced in this attitude by their CEOs, many of whom never darkened the door of a foundation staff room before they were hired to run one. As of this writing, most foundations are led by people with no prior experience in philanthropy; among even the fifty largest foundations, the number of experienced CEOs could be counted on the digits of two hands. Part of the blame for this situation can be laid at the door of executive search firms, which often seem to recycle for foundation openings failed candidates from searches in other fields, but ultimate responsibility rests with

foundation boards, which do not view philanthropic experience as an essential prerequisite for foundation leadership.
You would not want to entrust your car to the care of a person
who does not see himself as a mechanic, who does not stay current with the latest automotive techniques and technologies,
and who plans to leave the garage behind in a few months.
Why in the world, then, would you entrust hundreds of thousands or even millions of grant dollars to people with a dab-
bler's attitude toward grantmaking?

The extent to which too many people who make their living
in foundations consider themselves strangers in a strange land
is strikingly illustrated by the small handful of foundations that
express any interest—or place any grantmaking emphasis—on
the improvement of philanthropy. It is a curious phenomenon,
as self-loathing as if the Chamber of Commerce announced
that it had no interest in promoting the growth and development of business. As self-defeating as it is, however, it makes
perfect sense if people do not consider themselves to be grantmakers.

Foundation leaders need to eliminate this identity crisis.
While employed by a foundation, program officers—and
CEOs, for that matter—must take philanthropy *seriously*.
This means that they must define themselves first as grantmakers, not as members of some other profession who are
temporarily making grants. They must attend the meetings
and educational opportunities offered by the Council on
Foundations, the Association of Small Foundations, The
Grantmaking School, and their regional associations of grantmakers.[4] They must take the lessons learned in these meetings
and apply them to their craft, striving to improve the quality
of their own work and that of their foundation. It is surely not
too much to ask that people who are paid by foundations primarily dedicate their time and energy to making these foundations better servants of society.

OVERCOMING A CULTURE OF "BABBLE AND DABBLE"

Managing a foundation has been likened to herding cats, and some of the most vexing management problems arise from the tendencies just described within the foundation, which might be economically described as the problems of "babble and dabble." When all of the workforce have divergent training and experience, and their only common language is an incomprehensible jargon, the leader has to overcome the problem of babble. And when the workforce do not think of themselves primarily as grantmakers, and thus do not take grantmaking as seriously as they should, the leader has to overcome the problem of dabble.

These are serious problems, indeed, but they can be overcome if—and only if—foundation leaders are willing to meet the cultural challenge head on and to be more directive than they are usually comfortable being. Foundation leaders must insist on building a common culture, first by "de-babbleizing" communications, then by taking grantmaking seriously. Getting rid of babble requires an insistence on defining key terms and creating an Esperanto that is clear and understandable. As Tony Proscio archly notes, "New phrases and trendy or obscure coinages stick to foundations like briars to a long-haired dog. Unless someone carefully picks them out later, the poor beast hardly knows they're there."[5] Getting rid of dabble requires an insistence that all foundation employees put philanthropy first in their professional lives and strive constantly to improve their own work, along with that of the foundation itself.

Some foundations face a particularly large challenge in that the CEO is the babbler- and dabbler-in-chief. The chances of plain English being used, or professional development being an expectation, all but evaporate if the CEO is himself an incorrigible jargonizer and inveterate job-hopper. In such cases, boards of trustees must face up to the fact that a fish rots first from its head and must find new leadership that will take grant-making seriously.

If there ever was a time when it was sufficient for foundations to be run by babbling dilettantes dabbling in philanthropy while on temporary hiatus from their real careers, that time is long gone. To paraphrase Edmund Burke, "All that is required for the triumph of babble and dabble is for good foundation leaders to do nothing." In order for the triumph of clear communication and professionalism, however, foundation leaders must self-consciously build a common culture of clarity in communication and excellence in execution. This can be done only if leaders treat foundation management as seriously as they treat the social problems with which foundations grapple.

NOTES

1. Dwight McDonald, *The Ford Foundation: The Men and the Millions: An Unauthorized Biography* (New York: Reynal, 1956), 138–39.

2. Tony Proscio, *Bad Words for Good: How Foundations Garble Their Message and Lose Their Audience* (New York: Edna McConnell Clark Foundation, 2000); Tony Proscio, *In Other Words: A Plea for Plain Speaking in Foundations* (New York: Edna McConnell Clark Foundation, 2000).

3. Proscio, *In Other Words*, 29, 31, 46, 47.

4. The Council on Foundations, www.cof.org; Association of Small Foundations, www.smallfoundations.org; the Grantmaking School, www.grantmakingschool.org; the Forum of Regional Associations of Grantmakers (membership organization of the regional associations of grantmakers), www.givingforum.org.

5. Proscio, *In Other Words*, 8.

3

CHALLENGE 3: LACK OF A SALUTARY EXTERNAL DISCIPLINE

FOUNDATION FREEDOM: BLESSING OR CURSE?

Samuel Johnson memorably wrote, "Be dependent on it, Sir, when a man knows he is to be hanged in a fortnight, it concentrates his mind wonderfully." Foundation leaders, however, know that they are unlikely ever to be hanged, literally or even figuratively, so what can concentrate their minds? It may seem like a strange sentiment to bewail the field's lack of external threats, but just as a dangerous predator benefits the herd by culling the weak and the sick, external threats make organizations better. Foundations have no significant external threats, so what can provide them with the discipline needed to improve their performance?

Foundations are virtually alone among society's organizations in lacking such an external discipline. Commercial enterprises have a salutary external discipline called "the market." If a company does not effectively compete by offering goods or services that its customers want or can afford, the market will punish the company swiftly and brutally. Those corporations that learn lessons from the market prosper, while the landscape of commerce is littered with the carcasses of those that failed to learn fast enough.

In government, too, there is a salutary external discipline, called "the electorate." If a politician fails to adequately represent the wishes and desires of her constituents, she is likely to find herself, come the next election, on the underside of a landslide. Those who listen and learn, however, get reelected. Like bankruptcy in the commercial sector, electoral defeat in the government sector is rough, but highly effective, justice.

In most of the nonprofit sector, too, there is a salutary external discipline. If an environmental nonprofit, for example, is perceived as less effective than similar organizations, its constituents will turn to the more effective ones, both with their volunteer hours and their donations. The discipline may not be as swift or as brutal as that meted out by the market or the electorate, but it still benefits the nonprofit "herd" in the long run.

Only in the foundation world is there no salutary external discipline, or at least none powerful enough to compel foundation leaders' notice and respect. Foundations exist in a world with no effective competition, no customers as such, and no constituents. No matter how poorly a foundation performs, there is no chance that another funder will put it out of business, or that its applicants will boycott it, or that its grantees will vote the foundation's leaders out of office. Foundation leaders may not win any popularity contests, but no outside force can threaten their job security. And even though foundations are nonprofits, they are not (with the exception of community foundations) beholden to donors or volunteers, for their endowments cover all of their operating needs. Only a foundation's board of trustees provides oversight for its activities, so its CEO and officers naturally look inward, not outward, for their discipline.

Foundations, of course, are not devoid of legal oversight. Every one of them is subject to the laws and regulations of the federal government, as expressed through the Internal Revenue Code, and the laws and regulations of the state in which it is chartered, as expressed through that state's attorney general. This oversight, however, confers only minimal constraints upon foundations. These laws and regulations are mainly mechanical: they do not address quality of operation or effectiveness of outcomes. As long as a private foundation pays out 5 percent of its net asset value to eligible nonprofit grantees, for example, it has satisfied the Internal Revenue Service and its state's attorney general, even if all of the grants made were ill-advised and achieved no discernable positive impact.

All of this means that foundations, untroubled by the need to make a profit, unvexed by the need to please an electorate, unfettered by the need to raise operating funds, enjoy a distinctively high level of operational freedom. Functioning virtually without any external distractions, foundations are free to concentrate all of their energy on achieving their missions. That this extends a remarkable luxury to foundations no one will dispute, but there is considerably less agreement as to whether this freedom is a good thing, and how well they make use of it.

One school of thought holds that this lack of effective external discipline is a *blessing* to foundations. It allows them to support important social ventures that could never exist otherwise because they are unlikely ever to be profitable: so, foundations correct for market failures. It allows them to support important social issues that could not be voted into being because they are too controversial or benefit only a small minority: so, foundations correct for government failure. It allows them to kick-start new nonprofit ventures that are too far ahead of their time to get support from multiple small funders: so, foundations correct for fund-raising failure. Thus, the lack of external discipline *liberates* foundations to do what is risky, to do what is right, to do what is visionary, all without having to ask permission of bean counters, naysayers, and mossbacks. Foundations are America's social venture capital, social conscience, and social fund for the future.

A countervailing school of thought holds that this lack of effective external discipline is a *curse* to foundations. If foundations correct for market failure, then why do most of them make only short-term grants and constantly stress to their grantees the need to wean themselves from foundation support? If foundations correct for government failure, why have they been largely missing in action from the greatest social movements of the past century? (For example, only a handful of mainly smaller foundations, such as Field and Taconic, provided funding for the civil rights movement.) If they correct for fund-raising failure, why is it so difficult for new nonprofit ideas (those that don't fit preconceived requests for proposals) to get a fair hearing from program officers? Thus, the lack of external discipline *enervates* foundations, causing them to shy away from what is risky, right, and visionary, to play it safe so as to avoid criticism from bean counters, naysayers, and mossbacks. Foundations are America's wasted opportunity.

THE CURIOUS BEHAVIOR OF THE (FOUNDATION) DOG IN THE NIGHT-TIME

As usual, there is some truth on both sides of this divide. Partisans in either camp can certainly find, in the record of U.S. foundations, examples of grants both daring and craven, both conscientious and cynical, both visionary and shortsighted. Where does the truth ultimately lie? Perhaps the best place to search for it is in the Arthur Conan Doyle mystery "Silver Blaze," in which Sherlock Holmes remarks upon "the curious incident of the dog in the night-time." When Dr. Watson observes that "the dog did nothing in the night-time," Holmes replies, "That was the curious behavior."[1]

If foundations are indeed liberated by all of their freedom, if they are indeed boldly exercising it to correct the failures of the market, the government, and the fund-raisers, it would be virtually impossible to open a newspaper without reading of a groundbreaking social experiment fueled by their support. If this were the case, foundation-funded nonprofit organizations would be storming the barricades of homelessness, hunger, poverty, and undereducation, armed with flexibly funded, innovative, and effective grants. Like the dog in the Holmes story, however, foundations seem to be doing curiously little in the night-time. Barricades of homelessness, hunger, poverty, and undereducation remain intact, and those nonprofit organizations gallantly assaulting them constantly complain about the tepid support they receive from the nation's foundations. When foundations do appear in the papers, it is nearly always because their leaders have been caught doing something wrong: the *Boston Globe*, for example, has not run any series on highly effective grantmaking.

Defenders of the field will cry foul at using the media as the yardstick to judge foundations' use of their freedom. The press, they say, does not understand the intricacies of foundation work, and thus many quietly effective programs never appear in the papers. Moreover, the press cares only about the sensational and the negative, leaving on the cutting room floor stories about solid positive work done by foundation-funded programs. Doubtless, there is much truth to this analysis, and it does offer some measure of explanation for the silence of the dog in the night-time.

Even if, however, we accept all that the defenders offer to be true, we are left with the question of why the dog, if it has such enormous freedom, chooses to remain generally silent in the night-time. Foundations could lay siege to editorial boards, explaining the innovative work they have done and demonstrating the great results they have achieved, and demand more coverage for these pathbreaking outcomes, or at the very least, demand equal time with all the negative coverage. Foundations could do so, that is, if they *had* such great work and such wonderful outcomes to tout. If they have such results, the silence of the dog in the night-time is inexplicable. If they do not, that silence makes perfectly good sense.

So where does the needle of the balance ultimately point? Sadly, it points much nearer the side of enervation than that of liberation. This seeming paradox—the enigma of why unbridled freedom has produced such cautious behavior on the part of foundation leaders—has long puzzled even the most knowledgeable observers of the field. Jed Emerson, for example, says, "And I don't understand why people who clearly mean well and want to have an impact with the resources under their control are so hesitant to take some measure of higher value risk."[2]

The reason is actually very straightforward: *embarrassment.* Since foundations are undisciplined by the market, electorate, or funders, their only impetus for improvement comes from their (generally) self-perpetuating boards of trustees. If you are a foundation leader, your imperative thus is a simple one: keep the board happy, and you will keep your job. So, what makes a board happy? The answer is easy: pride-inducing success. What makes a board unhappy? The answer is equally easy: embarrassing failure. What does this mean for the CEO? As a practical matter, the answer to this question is also very simple: since any kind of success is preferable to any kind of failure, since embarrassing the board members is to be avoided at all costs, it is critically important that *every* project be a success. What is the best way to ensure that every project will be a success? The key to perpetual success is to keep every project uncomplicated and modest in its ambition. Thus, inexorably, in order to keep their boards happy, in order to assure that embarrassment never darkens the trustees' doorsteps, CEOs tend to seek the cautious and incremental success. Paradoxically, the societal organization given the most freedom to act hobbles itself; it is as if a superb French chef, capable of creating any gastronomic delight, insisted on making nothing except the blandest of oatmeal.

It is easy to point a finger of blame at timid, career-protecting chief executive officers, and CEOs, as a class, do deserve considerable censure. But Max King, the president of the Heinz Endowments in Pittsburgh, identified a broader problem upon becoming the chair of the Council on Foundations in 2006: "There is an old culture at foundations, an old culture in philanthropy, that tends to want to be quiet, cautious. . . . There are some factions . . . that are uncomfortable with being proactive, aggressive, and very public about their work."[3] Mr. King is certainly right about the antiquity of risk aversion in the foundation field. As long ago as 1956, Dwight McDonald, who is best remembered for his quip that "foundations are large bodies of money completely surrounded by people who want some,"[4] wrote in a far more serious vein that "large foundations, like large corporations, are timid beasts, and when they are frightened by some small but vocal minority, they envelop themselves in a cloud of public relations."[5] Whence arises all of this aversion to bold and decisive action? Largely, it springs from the most important of the factions mentioned by Mr. King, the CEO's bosses, the boards of trustees. It is to please boards, after all, that CEOs turn timorous. So what can be done to change this sad state of affairs? Quite simply, boards must redefine "failure" in the foundation context.

THE BLESSINGS OF FOUNDATION FAILURE

"Failure" in the foundation world is like chastity in the rest of the world: honored more in the breach than in the observance.

Newcomers to the field, whether executives or program officers, are routinely admonished that if every project is a success,
it means that the foundation is not being bold enough. Yet, as
Kenneth Prewitt of Columbia University notes:

> A foundation that does not fail is, presumably, not living up to
> its promise to explore what the market and the government shy
> away from. If a foundation were to take this promise seriously, it
> would announce what it believes to be the optimal ratio of pro-
> gram failure to program success and self-correct itself if it be
> came too risk-adverse. . . . to my knowledge, no American foun-
> dation justifies itself by calling attention to its program failures.[6]

No matter how much the concept of failure is publicly honored in the foundation world, in practice, foundation boards
treat failure as a scarlet letter and as a potential cause of embarrassing exposés in the media. To the board's way of thinking,
failure is failure, and it is better that their foundation be perceived as successful but not bold, rather than bold but occasionally unsuccessful. Thus the kudzu of mediocre success
creeps over foundations, strangling them under the sheer
weight of its repetition, choking out room for risk taking or true
innovation.

How can foundation boards clear the kudzu? The essential
first step is to distinguish between two very different kinds of
failure: sloppy and experimental. Sloppy failure occurs when
people fail to anticipate obvious obstacles, fail to plan for necessary contingencies, fail to develop incipient opportunities.
Sloppy failure is a result of human error, and if not for that error, the projects in question may have been successful. Experimental failure, on the other hand, occurs when despite all due
diligence, despite all thoughtful planning, despite all energetic
attempts at follow-through, the inherent challenges and un-
foreseeable side effects of a high-risk venture combine to cause
a negative outcome. Sloppy failure is to cause a plane crash by

forgetting to fill a fuel tank; experimental failure is to experience a plane crash while testing a new, promising, but untried
airplane.

The other key distinction between sloppy failure and experimental failure lies in the lessons that can be gleaned from them.
The only lesson that can be learned from sloppy failure is that
poor preparation and poor execution produce failure. Many
profound lessons can be learned from experimental failure,
each of which will help the foundation become more successful
in the future. The key, of course, is to evaluate experimental
failures rigorously, both to discover what went wrong and to
learn if those missteps can be corrected next time. A sloppy failure is just a failure, but an experimental failure is potentially a
step to ultimate success.

So what is a foundation's board to do—demand failure? The
answer is "yes." Not sloppy failure, of course, for no one wants
that. Boards, however, must demand a certain level of experimental failure, for that is the price of doing business in the nonprofit sector; the cost of true innovation; the payment for clear-
ing the kudzu of modest, incremental, "so what?" success. By
demanding occasional experimental failure, boards free foundation leaders from their self-imposed follow-through shackles.
If not every meal has to be perfect, the French chefs can abandon oatmeal and experiment with exotic new dishes.

Ironies abound in the management of foundations, but
nowhere more so than in this challenge. Just as the lack of external salutary disciplines has left foundations less free rather than
more, so it is necessary for foundation boards to impose the discipline of experimental failure upon foundation CEOs so that they
can ultimately experience significant success. Without the requirement of experimental failure, foundations will fall into the
trap of successes so small as to be meaningless, and leadership will
be so afraid of failing that they do not dare to succeed. It turns out
that when it comes to a foundation's freedom, Kris Kristofferson's

Bobby McGee got it right: "Freedom's just another word for nothin' left to lose."

NOTES

1. Arthur Conan Doyle, "Silver Blaze," in *The Memoirs of Sherlock Holmes* (Oxford: Oxford University Press, 1993), 23.

2. Jed Emerson, "Foundations: Essential and Missing in Action," *Alliance Extra*, March 2006, www.allvida.org/alliance/axmar06b .html?pnd (12 May 2006).

3. Max King, "Riskier Days Ahead for Stodgy Foundations," *Pittsburg Post-Gazette*.com, 7 May 2006, www.post-gazette.com/pg/pp/ 06127/688156.stm (12 May 2006).

4. Dwight McDonald, *The Ford Foundation: The Men and the Millions: An Unauthorized Biography* (New York: Reynal, 1956), 3.

5. McDonald, *The Ford Foundation*, 171.

6. Kenneth Prewitt, "American Foundations: What Justifies Their Unique Privileges and Powers," in *The Legitimacy of Philanthropic Foundations: U.S. and European Perspectives*, ed. Kenneth Prewitt, Mattei Dogan, Steven Heydemann, and Stefan Toepler (New York: Russell Sage Foundation, 2006), 35.

CHALLENGE 4: LACK OF RELIABLE FEEDBACK

FOUNDATION LEADERS: PRACTICALLY PERFECT IN EVERY WAY?

Ed Koch, New York City's mayor in the 1980s, incessantly asked a single question while on the campaign trail: "How'm I doin'?" And, since Gothamites were not shy about candidly answering that question, Mayor Koch always had an excellent idea of where he stood with his constituents. This feedback-rich environment had its moments of misery, but overall it worked well for His Honor, for he served three terms as mayor of the nation's largest city.

Foundation leaders, by sharp contrast, live in a feedback-poor environment. Their virtually unchecked power to decline grant requests explains why few applicants or grantees are brave enough—or foolhardy enough—to criticize their faults and shortcomings. It is also only natural that many applicants and grantees are crafty enough—or wise enough—to praise and flatter them shamelessly. This gusher of praise and drought of criticism is pleasant, especially for leaders who come to foundations from the unpleasantness of feedback-rich environments, but it does nothing to help them gauge their performance and in fact tends to promote wholly unwarranted smugness and self-satisfaction.

Mayor Koch's question was more than just a parlor exercise, for reliable feedback keeps people and organizations in touch with external reality. Most professions exist in feedback-rich environments. Elementary school teachers, for example, receive much direct, even tactless, commentary on their performance, as do salespeople, coaches, and nurses. Some of the feedback is unwarranted and even infuriating, but all of it provides valuable data that help these professionals understand what they are doing well, identify flaws, and increase effectiveness. In such feedback-rich professions, there are ample opportunities for the practitioners to receive direct input on their performance. Until recently, there was simply no such mechanism in the foundation world.

In fact, for years, foundation leaders pooh-poohed the notion of seeking feedback at all (some, unfortunately, still do). They looked upon it as the ultimate fool's errand, for naturally any applicant who had been turned down would complain bitterly about the process and the decision, while any successful grantee would find both the process and the decision to be fair and wise. What could be learned from this dynamic, they asked, other than that declining requests disappointed people, and funding requests delighted people? No, evaluation under such circumstances was mere navel-gazing, an unwise expenditure of time and money in order to grasp the utterly obvious.

So foundation employees at all levels lived in a cheerful, if opaque, bubble in which flattery was commonplace and criticism rarely intruded. The more self-aware among them realized that much of the flattery was unearned, and there was considerable unarticulated dissatisfaction among applicants, and even among grantees. These hardy souls did their best to appropriately discount the flattery and encourage honest feedback. There were, however, plenty of less self-aware foundation leaders who reveled in the praise, accepting it at face value, and even, in extreme cases, coming to expect it as their due. As Peter Frumkin notes, "Few nonprofits are able to express themselves candidly . . . even if they have major complaints and concerns."[1] Nor did they question the absence of criticism, regarding it as solid evidence of the high quality of their interactions with applicants and grantees. Among this group, the result of the dearth of reliable feedback was a completely misplaced sense of worth: "I'm good, and I have the data to prove it, for I get nothing but compliments."

Thus arose the caricature of the foundation leader, his every move a royal progress, his thirst for fulsome praise unslakable, his aversion to even the mildest criticism absolute. The more out of touch and ineffective he became, the firmer grew his belief that he was a paragon of effectiveness. He was "large and in charge," the "sage on the stage," and secretly, the butt of every joke when applicants (and even grantees) gathered together. Waldemar Nielsen, an exemplary practitioner and perceptive critic of the field, notes that although a program officer "may receive public flattery, he is commonly held in private disrespect by those with whom he has professional dealings."[2] They would say of him, as Winston Churchill once said of a rival in the House of Commons, "There, but for the grace of God, goes God."

BURSTING THE BUBBLE OF FOUNDATION SMUGNESS

Sunshine, as everyone knows, is the best disinfectant, but how is the sunshine of reliable feedback to be introduced into this dark bubble of foundation smugness? A pioneering effort to let the sunshine in was launched in the late 1980s when the Joseph & Edna Josephson Institute of Ethics undertook a research project designed to gauge ethical standards for both grantmakers and grantseekers. The Institute discovered striking discrepancies between the perceptions of the respective camps. For instance, in response to the question "You would rate the ethics of foundation trustees or board members as . . . ," 63 percent of a sample of grantmakers answered either "excellent" or "very good," while a mere 12 percent of grantseekers gave such high marks. Only 5 percent of the grantmakers rated the ethics of foundation leaders as "fair" or "poor," while 36 percent of grantseekers did (and another 4 percent rated them "very poor").[3] The Josephson Institute research certainly exposed the vast gulf between the rosy self-perceptions of grantmakers and the much harsher views of applicants and grantees. It would be wrong, however, to say that this pioneering effort had much of an impact upon the field. Although the results were published in a book, *Ethics in Grantmaking and Grantseeking*, it was not widely distributed, and the Josephson findings were neither well noted nor long remembered by foundation leaders.

A decade after the Josephson experiment, a handful of individual foundations, such as Packard and Kellogg, tried their hands at surveying their own grantees, and even applicants whose requests they had declined. The results were mixed but generally more encouraging than the Josephson findings. The self-administered nature of the surveys, however, raised questions about the validity of the results, for even though respondents had been assured of anonymity, they feared severe reprisals if foundation employees inferred their identities from their responses. Thoughtful leaders of these foundations, therefore, tended to discount the accuracy of their own data.

It was not until 2003, when the Center for Effective Philanthropy began to offer foundations their Grantee Perception Report, that the prospect for truly candid and reliable feedback became a reality. The Center, a neutral third party, guarantees the anonymity of grantee respondents (foundation employees do not see the raw data) and thus encourages candid responses. As of June 2006, the Center had generated 102 Grantee Perception Reports for all types and sizes of foundations. The grantees' perceptions of the interactions with foundations during the grantmaking process, and the impact of the foundations' actions, have proved an eye-opening experience to the foundations commissioning the reports. Fully 97 percent of the participating foundations have made operational changes on the basis of what they have learned from the survey, according to an evaluation conducted by LaFrance Associates, LLC. Actions taken by the foundations range from major changes in grantmaking strategy to improvements in grantmaking processes and communications with grantees.[4] The *Chronicle of Philanthropy* concluded that the Grantee Perception Reports "have resulted in changes in foundation operations and have fostered a frank dialogue between grantmakers and charities, which historically have been wary of speaking out against their supporters for fear of losing money."[5]

There can be no doubt that the Center for Effective Philanthropy's Grantee Perception Report constitutes a great leap forward in the quest for reliable external feedback in the foundation world. Foundations, for the first time, are able to get unvarnished responses from an uncowed sampling of their "customers." The Center for Effective Philanthropy has recently launched a second series of assessments, the Applicant Perception Report, focusing on the perceptions of applicants whose proposals were declined by foundations, so both successful and unsuccessful requesters can now be heard. These constructive data provide the basis for real foundation improvement.[6] On the other hand, neither the Grantee Perception Report nor the Applicant Perception Report in themselves provide a sufficient solution to the feedback challenge. To date, fewer than one-sixth of 1 percent of American foundations have commissioned a Grantee Perception Report. The report is too expensive for every foundation to pursue, and in any case, the Center lacks the capacity to conduct them for all 80,000 American foundations.

Clearly, a less expensive and more accessible way to garner un-biased feedback must be found, perhaps through the growing network of university centers for the study of philanthropy.

THE ROAD TO FOUNDATION IMPROVEMENT

The Center for Effective Philanthropy has, however, opened wide the door to honest feedback, and more foundations should walk through it. Individual foundations can and should take more vigorous steps to openly court such feedback and put it to use. Tom David has suggested several practical steps founda-tions can take to solicit useful information, such as convening grantees in retreat settings or conferences; conducting trans-parent grantee surveys, focus groups, and phone interview sur-veys; distributing mail-back cards; and creating a habit of lis-tening closely to all stakeholders. David further suggests that foundations should actively encourage their staffs to reflect on the data thus collected, as well as create group learning forums so that employees absorb the lessons and put them to use. Foundations should publish the results on their websites and in their annual reports, and likewise share with their stakeholders and with the broader field the lessons they have learned and the adjustments in practice that they intend to make as a result.[7]

However it is done, it must be done. As legendary Penn State football coach Joe Paterno once remarked, "You're either getting better, or you're getting worse." There is no status quo, only evo-lution—or devolution. Either foundations are making proactive efforts to improve through careful evaluation of external feed-back and thoughtful course corrections, or they are getting worse. Foundation leaders need to do more to get better, and they need to do it soon. There is no excuse for organizations with so much freedom and so many resources to behave so arbitrar-ily and so thoughtlessly toward their "customers'" needs and wants, and most of all, with no justification for the lousy performance that such heedlessness inevitably brings in its train.

The benefits of listening carefully to applicants and grantees alike are nicely summarized by the Center for Effective Philanthropy:

> Ultimately, the beneficiaries of better foundation-grantee relationships are not just grantees and foundations, but the people and issues they seek to affect through their work. By working more productively together, foundations and grantees can create more positive social impact. This, after all, is the ultimate goal of both parties.[5]

NOTES

1. Peter Frumkin, "Accountability and Legitimacy in American Foundation Philanthropy," in *The Legitimacy of Philanthropic Foundations: U.S. and European Perspectives*, ed. Kenneth Prewitt, Mattei Dogan, Steven Heydemann, and Stefan Toepler (New York: Russell Sage Foundation, 2006), 106.

2. Waldemar A. Nielsen, *The Big Foundations* (New York: Columbia University Press, 1972), 327.

3. Michael Josephson, *Ethics in Grantmaking and Grantseeking: Making Philanthropy Better* (Marina Del Rey, CA: Joseph & Edna Josephson Institute of Ethics, 1992), 152.

4. Center for Effective Philanthropy, "Assessment Tools: Grantee Perception Report," Center for Effective Philanthropy, www.effective philanthropy.org/assessment/assessment_gpr.html (5 June 2006).

5. Ian Wilhelm, "Giving Charities a Voice: Organization Offers Foundations an Unvarnished Evaluation," *Chronicle of Philanthropy*, 17, 10 November 2005.

6. Center for Effective Philanthropy, "Assessment Tools: Applicant Perception Report," Center for Effective Philanthropy, www.effective philanthropy.org/assessment/assessment_apr.html (5 June 2006).

7. Tom David, "Ready, Set, Learn: The Foundation as a Learning Organization" (July 2006 *Learning*), Grantmakers for Effective Organizations, www.geofunders.org/index.cfm?fuseaction=page.viewPage&pageID=431&rodeID=1 (17 July 2006).

8. Kevin Bolduc, Phil Buchanan, and Judy Huang, *What Nonprofits Value in Their Foundation Funders* (New York: Center for Effective Philanthropy, 2004), 3.

CHALLENGE 5: LACK OF AN ACCEPTED BODY OF GOOD PRACTICES

WHO IS GOOD? WHO IS BAD? WHO CAN SAY?

Most foundation leaders cherish ambitions to constantly improve the performance of their organizations. A formidable obstacle stands in their path, however, namely a persistent difficulty in articulating just what "better" means in the foundation context. Although the first modern U.S. charitable foundation, the Peabody Education Fund, was established in 1867, the field remains loosely connected, more like an ancient league of city-states than a modern profession. It has few unifying forces, many petty rivalries, and very little consensus around fundamental issues that it faces. As a result, even such basic questions as how long it should take a foundation to make a yes or no decision on a grant request simply have no consistent answer from foundation to foundation.

It is a paradox that the foundation field could have been with us for so long, have developed so much, and yet have come to agree upon so little. After the initial impetus provided by Peabody, the great general-purpose foundations, the Carnegie

Corporation (1911) and the Rockefeller Foundation (1913), appeared early in the twentieth century and scored great successes in battles to roll back diseases and improve higher education. By the middle of the twentieth century, an infrastructure of professionalism began to appear, with the establishment of the Council on Foundations in 1949 and the Foundation Center in 1956. The Tax Reform Act of 1969 eliminated the worst of the unprofessional practices from the field. And yet, in spite of all of this history and evolution, the field remains curiously and stubbornly averse to unifying or even organizing principles. As the old saw goes, "If you've seen one foundation, you've seen one foundation."

Many a foundation employee has felt the sting of such arbitrariness. One program officer of my acquaintance, who won a Scrivner Award for creativity in grantmaking from the Council on Foundations while working for a small foundation, was criticized for being *too* creative when she later went to work for a larger foundation. It was not that her grantmaking had changed; rather, what had been celebrated as creativity in the smaller foundation was perceived as a lack of teamwork in the larger one. A hard lesson for program officers is that, in the absence of fieldwide standards, good grantmaking is whatever your boss of the moment says it is.

From time to time, this phenomenon erupts into a mass exodus of the staff after a new CEO is installed. The appointments of Michael Bailin as CEO of the Edna McConnell Clark Foundation in 1996; of Carl J. Schramm as CEO of the Ewing Marion Kauffman Foundation in 2002; and of Judith Rodin as CEO of the Rockefeller Foundation in 2005 all resulted in turnovers among the program staff approaching 50 percent of the total. Were these cases of neo-Stalinist purges of talented people based on personality conflicts, or was it desperately needed pruning of deadwood? Given the current absence of criteria for excellence in the field, these questions cannot be answered with objective certainty.

How does the leadership of the field feel about this "standardless" existence? Pose this question to them, and their answers tend to mirror that of Americans when asked what they think of the United States Congress: "The Congress as a whole is a dreadful mess, but my representative is a fine fellow." Foundation leaders clearly see the flawed performance of other foundations, but they are generally satisfied that their own organizations are performing well. In fact, the widespread perception that "all foundations except mine are subpar" only serves to confirm that the lack of standards makes it impossible to definitively distinguish good practice from bad in the foundation world.

This state of affairs is in sharp contrast to the conditions prevailing in other fields. For example, in the museum profession, there is a long-established system of peer-reviewed accreditation, administered by the American Association of Museums (AAM), according to standards developed by museum professionals themselves. Individual museums seeking accreditation are provided with the standards of practice they must meet, and the AAM offers a preaccreditation program to help the applying museum achieve these stringent requirements. A rigorous peer review qualifies—or disqualifies—the museum for accreditation. After passing the test, the museum must continue to abide by the standards and must submit to periodic reaccreditation in order to keep its credentials current.

The AAM accreditation process is a rigorous one, to be sure, but its effect is to guarantee a high level of professional performance from museums that make the grade. It also sets a standard of excellence toward which nonaccredited museums can strive. The most profound benefits of accreditation, however, are not those garnered by museums but rather those that accrue for the audiences museums serve. Their museum-going experience is enhanced by high standards of object collection, preservation, and exhibition, as well as by first-rate educational programs. Accreditation in the museum field, in short, is the rising tide that lifts all boats.

There is no comparable policy of accreditation in the foundation world, nor is there a strong groundswell of support for initiating one. As Kenneth Prewitt has archly noted:

> There has been some interest in peer review to strengthen the accountability of foundations, modeled on the accreditation systems used by higher education in the United States. Depending on its design, such a system could move closer to substantive accountability—and perhaps for that reason it has remained an issue for discussion in scholarly journals more than an active topic among foundation trustees and officers.[1]

In the absence of standards, what yardstick can be used to separate high-performing from low-performing foundations? One possible criterion is membership in the Council on Foundations or the Association of Small Foundations. Presumably, foundations belonging to these trade associations benefit from programs of education and mutual aid and become higher-performing institutions. In fact, the Council on Foundations has published its own set of principles and practices for good grantmaking, as have some regional associations of grantmakers.[2]

These standards, however, are rarely put into the hands of new program officers, due to the training gap described in chapter 1. As a result, no reliable data exist to demonstrate that members of foundation trade associations have created better practices or achieved more encouraging outcomes than have nonmembers. Even if member foundations were superior performers, however, it would by no means result in universal—or even widespread—improvement in the field, for more than 90 percent of all foundations belong to neither the Council on Foundations nor the Association of Small Foundations.

GOOD PRACTICES OR GOOD LUCK?

Another possible yardstick that could be used to identify high-performing foundations is the results that flow from the projects they fund. If the outcomes are good, the foundation must be employing good practices to make its grants, and if the outcomes are bad, it must be the result of bad grantmaking practices. There can be no doubt that this is sometimes true, but there can also be no doubt that sometimes it is correlation, not causation, that links practices and outcomes. It sometimes happens that foundations with indifferent practices of due diligence and burdensome systems for applicants and grantees alike nonetheless fund projects with excellent outcomes. It also sometimes happens that foundations with exemplary due diligence practices and applicant/grantee-friendly systems nonetheless fund projects with lousy outcomes.

For example, during the 1980s, the Gannett Foundation was one of the nation's most respected corporate foundations. Then Al Neuharth, the chairman of the Gannett Company, retired from that role and took leadership of the foundation. The hard-charging Neuharth, who had defied naysayers by creating the first national news daily, *USA Today*, approached his grantmaking in an autocratic style, spending extravagantly on the foundation's new headquarters in Virginia and strategically buying enough copies of his own autobiography, *Confessions of an SOB*, to land it on the *New York Times* bestseller list. Neuharth eventually changed the name of the foundation to the Freedom Forum and focused on a bulletproof cause: the First Amendment to the Constitution. The Freedom Forum threw its resources into the creation of the first museum dedicated to freedom of expression, and the "Newseum" has proved to be a great success. Despite the fact that "self-serving generosity has been the hallmark of the Forum and Neuharth,"[3] and despite the fact that the Newseum was created at least partly as a public relations enhancer, the outcomes of these grants have succeeded in promoting the cause of free expression.

Conversely, in 1991, the Chicago Community Trust and local partners began three years of planning prior to launching a multiyear program named the Children, Youth and Families Initiative (CYFI), a daunting attempt to support the developmental needs of children and families in seven Chicago neighborhoods by integrating and broadening the social services that helped sustain them. CYFI proved to be an extremely complex project, and it encountered a good deal of organizational inertia and strong bureaucratic resistance. As Joel Fleishman notes, "It was a reasonable concept, but . . . quickly deteriorated into a series of power struggles with community groups, draining its effectiveness and reducing its impact."[4] If one judged solely from the outcomes, one would guess that the Newseum was funded by a foundation that was very inclusive in its grantmaking, while CYFI was supported by a foundation that was arbitrary in its grantmaking, but the facts are just the opposite. By their results, then, ye shall not (necessarily) know them.

HEALING A SELF-INFLICTED WOUND

The lack of an accepted body of good practices in the foundation world presents a challenge, but it is a challenge with a solution. Just as the AAM devised a peer-driven system of accreditation for museum professionals, so could the Council on Foundations (or the Association of Small Foundations) do so for the foundation field. If accreditation proves too ambitious a goal, at least its precursor—a body of widely recognized good practices—would be worth developing for its own sake. There certainly is no shortage of organizations that can contribute the talent and resources that would be necessary to generate a body of good practices. The Center for Effective Philanthropy is amassing, through its Grantee and Applicant Perception Reports, a vast trove of data on effective operation. Grantmakers for Effective Organizations has been studying the components of grantmaker effectiveness for more than five years and has a wealth of solid information on its website. The Grantmaking School and the GrantCraft initiative have significant data on good practice and solid experience in teaching these practices to foundation program officers.[5] These information resources, of course, could be instantly mobilized by the financial wherewithal that foundations command. The only missing components, indeed, are widespread recognition of the need for generally accepted principles of good practice and the political will necessary to create and sustain a process that would lead to the creation of a fieldwide body of such principles.

Until the happy day when those components materialize, the foundation field will continue on its "weird sisters" course, in which "fair is foul and foul is fair," a course in which no one is excellent and no one is awful, because no one can definitively say exactly what is excellent and what is awful. Standard-free philanthropy was inevitable in the cradle days of organized giving. In the infinitely better-organized twenty-first-century foundation field, standard-free philanthropy is a roadblock to the field's effectiveness. It is a roadblock, however, that can and must be addressed soon. The alternative to action by foundations in the field is action taken by outsiders—such as the United States Congress—to impose standards on foundations. Even in a standardless field, that is one practice that all can agree is undesirable.

NOTES

1. Kenneth Prewitt, "American Foundations: What Justifies Their Unique Privileges and Powers," in *The Legitimacy of Philanthropic*

Foundations: U.S. and European Perspectives, ed. Kenneth Prewitt, Mattei Dogan, Steven Heydemann, and Stefan Toepler (New York: Russell Sage Foundation, 2006), 44.

2. Council on Foundations, "Principles and Practices for Effective Grantmaking," www.cof.org/Learn/content.cfm?ItemNumber=776 (21 September 2006).

3. Russ Baker, "Cracks in a Foundation: The Freedom Forum Narrows its Vision," *Columbia Journalism Review*, www.cjr.org/issues/2002/1/cracks-baker.asp? (19 September 2006).

4. Joel Fleishman, *The Foundation: A Great American Secret: How Private Wealth Is Changing the World* (New York: PublicAffairs, 2007), 205.

5. www.effectivephilanthropy.org; www.geofunders.org; www.grant makingschool.org; www.grantcraft.org.

CHALLENGE 6: LACK OF IDEOLOGICAL COHESION BETWEEN BOARD AND STAFF

WE HAVE MET THE ENEMY, AND IT IS OUR COLLEAGUES

Newly elected members of Congress soon learn—to their surprise—that the *real* opposition does not come from the party across the aisle; no, the real opposition comes from the other chamber in the Capitol building. The dynamic of House versus Senate in Congress is analogous to the dynamic of staff versus board in foundations. The Constitution's framers meant to divide power between a House that represented the popular will and a Senate that provided a brake on their desires. Whether they mean to or not, those who establish foundations create the same check-and-balance system between a staff that interacts with applicants and grantees and a board of trustees that serves as a skeptical audience for staff recommendations. Hence, if you were to ask the staff of most foundations about their most formidable obstacle, their response would not be "poverty," or "disease," but rather "my board." Similarly, most board members, if asked the same question, would answer "our program officers." This is not true of every staffed foundation, but it is so—or at least perceived by the protagonists to be so—in a goodly number of them.

This staff versus board fissure has, like the heroine of a Victorian novel, a cloud of pervasive gloom hanging over it. Foundations can be established only by people who have made a considerable amount of money, and mostly this money comes from having created or managed a successful business enterprise. When they establish their foundations, the donors tend to choose as trustees their friends and business associates, people who come from the same socioeconomic class as themselves, who might efficiently be described as the well bred, well fed, and well read. Having prospered in the existing system, board members tend to be averse to dismantling it and are often skeptical even of significantly reforming it. As Kenneth Prewitt notes, "Private capital accumulation in very large amounts and the substantial economic inequality that results is simply not viewed by wealthy philanthropists and the successor trustees as a root cause of the social maladies that are there to be ameliorated."[1]

Program officers, by and large, are cut from different fabric, usually with more modest means, and are often fresh from direct engagement in the battles against hunger, disease, ignorance, and poverty. Thus they are acutely aware of the inequities and inefficiencies of the existing system. Program officers, therefore, tend to be as keen to reform the system as board members are to preserve it.

The check-and-balance analogy breaks down, however, on the issue of the power dynamic. Unlike the House and Senate, each of which has power and prerogatives, in foundations, boards have power and staffs answer to them. This creates an "us versus them" dynamic, and the conflict is only exacerbated by the setting in which board members and program officers typically interact: that highly charged atmosphere of the board meeting, in which the program officers recommend projects for funding. For the program officer, the stakes are very high. Months of work are on the line, beginning with a letter of intent or request for proposals, then extensive due diligence, guiding the applicant through the process of writing the proposal and navigating the proposal through the internal approvals process leading up to the board meeting. In the course of this journey, the program officer often becomes a passionate believer in the applicant and its mission, so she comes to the meeting as an outright advocate. For the board members, too, the stakes are very high. The donor's intention and the foundation's reputation are on the line with every grant it makes, and the trustee feels this responsibility acutely. The program officer's passion collides with the board member's caution, occasionally in open conflict but frequently in coded language, with an undercurrent of mutual suspicion, suppressed emotions, and smoldering resentment. Repeated board meetings in this mode result in the development of an unhealthy pattern in which the board members may come to regard the program officers as unabashed shills for projects both good and marginal, and in some cases as closet socialists who never met an anticapitalist ideologue that they didn't like, while program officers may come to regard board members as so many potholes in the road to progress, and in some cases as reflexive reactionaries who are forever trying to thwart the reform of broken systems.

THE CEO: THE MONKEY IN THE MIDDLE?

With the staff generally entrenched on the left wing, and boards generally in a redoubt on the right wing, the CEO finds himself occupying the no-man's land in between. His thankless task is to transform that space into common ground. It is a delicate and never-ending dance, one that has deeply furrowed the face of many a foundation chief executive. Typically, the tactics CEOs choose to reduce the conflict between board and staff are effective, but they cause considerable collateral damage to the foundation by amplifying the previously discussed problems of obfuscation and risk aversion.

Any observant foundation CEO quickly notes that there are certain terms or phrases that evoke a visceral reaction among selected board members. It could be words such as *gender*, *quota*, or *equity*, or phrases such as *social justice, public policy*, or *living wage*. I once made the mistake in a board meeting of attempting to underline the nonpartisan approach of a youth service applicant organization by stating that it counted among its supporters both archconservative senator Jesse Helms of North Carolina and ultraliberal senator Edward Kennedy of Massachusetts. One trustee literally came out of his seat and fumed, "If Teddy Kennedy is for it, then I'm against it." Only an extensive (and extemporaneous) intervention by the foundation's president prevented this million-dollar request from being declined, solely on the basis of one trustee's intemperate response to the mention of one person's name.

The lesson that foundation CEOs take from incidents such as these is that the board member objects more to the word or phrase itself than to the actions described by these words. Therefore, if one simply replaces such "third rail" words (touch them, and your first symptom is death) with innocuous synonyms, it is usually possible to pass the request pretty much intact. Hence, if a board member strenuously objects to any request that includes "public policy" in the title, simply replace those offensive words with "civil society formation educational programming," and the trustee's objection goes away. Just as George Carlin had a list of the "seven words you cannot say on TV," most foundation CEOs have a significantly longer list of words that program officers cannot use in communicating with board members.

From the CEO's perspective, it is always better to "euphemize" than to "euthanize"—that is, to replace the "hot button words" and pass a recommendation, as opposed to leaving them in and seeing the recommendation go down in flames. As effective as that may be, the tendency to euphemize has one unfortunate side effect: it promotes the use of a particularly noxious form of the "foundationese" discussed in chapter 2: jargon deliberately coined to obfuscate rather than to clarify.

The second double-edged tactic used by CEOs to defuse board-staff tensions is even more effective, but it is also considerably more damaging to the foundation. The CEO notices that certain board members object vociferously to recommendations that carry a significant level of risk. The board members feel that failure, even of the most honorable variety, will expose the foundation to ridicule, so they seek to minimize risk at all costs. The foundation's CEO, therefore, pounces on chance-taking wherever it can be found, blocking program officers from bringing forward projects with high risk–high reward ratios. Board-staff relations are definitely improved as risk goes down, but the foundation, as discussed in chapter 3, is condemned to a string of insipid successes that produce no real impact upon society. This systematic wringing out of risk by foundation leaders rightly bothers many thoughtful observers of the foundation world. Susan Raymond, for example, asks plaintively, "Is that what philanthropy is supposed to be? Are we mortgage brokers, or are we visionaries?"[2]

A POX UPON EXPERIENCE

The clash of cultures between board and staff also has another subtle long-term legacy for the foundation world: the curious negative effect that field experience has upon career advancement. As noted in chapter 1, most foundation boards do not hire people with experience in the foundation field to fill top leadership positions, especially that of CEO. In most professions, of course, experience is an absolute prerequisite for professional advancement. It is difficult to imagine an accounting firm, for example, choosing a non-CPA as its chief executive. At many foundations, however, significant foundation experience seems to actually disqualify people from promotion to top jobs. One reason for this curious behavior is found in the dynamic of board-staff interaction discussed earlier in this chapter.

Board members want CEOs who will give them the straight scoop, the unvarnished truth, leaders who will always admit that there is an elephant in the middle of the room. What they have gotten from program officers over the years is sales jobs—sometimes, in their view, snow jobs—and an endless litany of euphemism and obfuscation. Hiring such people to run their foundation would be like hiring Eddie Haskell of *Leave It to Beaver* fame: an apparently clean-cut fellow whose earnest apple polishing around adults covered a fundamentally deceitful nature. Placing a Haskell-like rascal in charge of their foundation would be a deeply irresponsible act; hence they turn to outsiders instead.

The fundamental problem with this practice is that, again and again, it leads boards to hire an amateur to do a professional's job. Board members will counter that seasoned executives from other fields have a world of translatable experience, pointing to iconic foundation presidents such as David Hamburg, who came from the academy, and Alan Pifer, who came from the world of business. These great leaders, however, are the scarce exceptions, not the rule. For every Hamburg or Pifer, there are a dozen like Richard Lyman, Barry Munitz, and Al Neuharth, whose tenures were marred by mediocrity, scandal, or regression. Foundation boards can hire any sort of professional they please, but those who have labored long and learned much in philanthropy's vineyards rarely please them. Veteran program officers, who have worked for one eminent but amateurish CEO after another, often adapt the old quip about education to explain why their foundation is faltering and failing: "It's not the school that's bad; it's just the principal of the thing."

THE BALL IS IN THE BOARD'S COURT

The gulf that divides a foundation's staff and board will always be with us, but there are ways to bridge gulfs. Staff will always propose, and boards will always dispose, and that means the program officers will always be in the position of selling ideas to the board. That much cannot be helped. What can be improved, however, is the way in which the transaction is handled. Board members must understand that in the unequal power dynamic of the foundation, they are proactive, while program officers are reactive. Hence, board members are directly responsible for many of the staff's behaviors that annoy them most. Program officer obfuscation, to take just one, happens as the direct result of one or more board members exploding like Krakatoa in reaction to hearing controversial words or concepts. Similarly, program officers' repeated hyping of mediocre programs is virtually foreordained by those board members who pounce on risky recommendations as if they were weasels in a henhouse. In short, boards get the kinds of relationship with program officers that they create, and then, ironically, cite that relationship as the reason for hiring amateurs to run their foundations.

Since the problem is of the board's making, the solution must be of the board's creation. As Edward Skloot, former CEO of the Surdna Foundation, correctly notes, "Those with power should act first."[3] Often, the problem begins at the very birth of the foundation, when the donor chooses trustees based not on how much experience or knowledge or creativity they can bring to the table, but rather based upon friendship or a preexisting professional relationship. College roommates, personal attorneys, trusted accountants, and tennis doubles partners may all be wonderful people, but whether they will make effective foundation board members is another question entirely. Donors need to ask the key question, "Will this candidate for board membership make a thoughtful, productive trustee?" not "Will I be personally comfortable with this person?"

Whether the donor is still active, or if successor trustees are in charge, the careful selection of new board members based on ability, as opposed to affability, is absolutely essential to good governance. So is self-policing of behavior. Typically, it is a small minority of a foundation's board members who turn rabid upon reading buzzwords or ride roughshod over any proposal involving appreciable risk. The problem is not so much the fact that such board members exist as it is that the board's constructive members suffer in silence while these feckless few are throwing tantrums. It is never pleasant, of course, to rebuke one's fellow trustees, but the constructive majority must do so in order to choke off the staff's obfuscation at its source.

The ideological differences between board and staff are a tougher nut to crack, but not an impossible one. It is enormously important that these differences get aired out and made explicit. The board must clarify just how much social change they can stand and how much is too much. Again, though, the board must take the lead, and this, unfortunately, is not currently a common practice in the field. The Center for Effective Philanthropy has found that very few foundation boards engage in systematic self-assessment of their own effectiveness.[4] So it is high time that foundation boards turn the spotlight upon themselves and seek to consciously improve their own performance. In fact, it is not too much to say that significant staff improvement is not possible without the board improving itself first.

To be fair, foundation staff members must do their part to help their boards become more effective. Board members are busy people, and the last thing they have time for is what foundation staffs typically give them: a veritable blizzard of briefings and board book materials. The Center for Effective Philanthropy discovered that 52 percent of the board members it surveyed complained of receiving too much material, which explains why only 48 percent of them reported that they read all of the materials. One exasperated trustee actually weighed the material sent and discovered that it amounted to seven pounds for a single meeting![5] So when program officers complain, as they frequently do, that board members did not even bother to read the materials they prepared, there is often a reason—or, more precisely, seven pounds of reasons.

If donors continue to create "best friends" boards, if these boards remain reluctant to improve, and if staffs continue to contribute to their ineffectiveness, the results will be continued obfuscation, mediocrity, and amateurism. These are not scarlet sins—indeed, to paraphrase Carl Sandburg—the sins of foundations are dishwater gray. Until their boards take the lead on improving the relationship with their staffs; until their boards come to understand that experience in philanthropy does have value; and until their boards realize that foundations should be led by people who know, understand, and believe in them, the sins of foundations are likely to remain the color of dishwater. This is truly a damning indictment for organizations endowed with so much and capable of doing so much for so many.

NOTES

1. Kenneth Prewitt, "American Foundations: What Justifies Their Unique Privileges and Powers," in *The Legitimacy of Philanthropic Foundations: U.S. and European Perspectives*, ed. Kenneth Prewitt, Mattei Dogan, Steven Heydemann, and Stefan Toepler (New York: Russell Sage Foundation, 2006), 34.

2. Susan Raymond, "American Philanthropy and the Twenty-first Century: A Plea for the World of Ideas," *On Philanthropy 2005*, onphilanthropy.com/articles/print.aspx?cid=744 (8 December 2005).

3. Edward Skloot, "Slot Machines, Boat Building, and the Future of Philanthropy," *Responsive Philanthropy: The NCRP Quarterly* (Spring 2002): 15.

4. Phil Buchanan, Kevin Bolduc, and Debbie Liao, *Toward a Common Language: Listening to Foundation CEOs and Other Experts Talk about Performance Measurement in Philanthropy* (Boston: Center for Effective Philanthropy, 2002), 12.

5. Phil Buchanan, Ellie Buteau, Sarah Di Troia, and Romero Hayman, *Beyond Compliance: The Trustee Viewpoint on Effective Foundation Governance: A Report on Phase II of the Center for Effective Philanthropy's Foundation Governance Project* (Boston: Center for Effective Philanthropy, 2005), 15.

7

CHALLENGE 7: LACK OF IDEOLOGICAL COHESION WITHIN THE STAFF

FOUNDATIONS: PHILANTHROPIC YUGOSLAVIA?

In the previous chapter, the focus was on the lack of ideological cohesion between the foundation's board and its staff. As important as the board is to a foundation, however, it is but a part-time presence; in only a small handful of foundations do boards meet more often than quarterly. When the boards decamp for home after their meetings, the staff remains, the biggest single factor that unifies the staff disappears, and the lack of ideological cohesion within the staff itself comes again to the fore.

It is tempting, if perhaps a bit overblown, to compare a foundation's staff to the former nation of Yugoslavia and to say that instead of Serbs, Bosnians, and Croatians, foundations have program officers, financial officers, and administrators. The comparison is exaggerated, of course, because the factions in foundations don't actually try to kill each other, but there are nonetheless some parallels along the lines of ancient grudges, simmering feuds, and irrational rivalries. Many (if not most) organizations have a defining or dominant culture that provides a common ground for its disparate components. Foundations, with their amateur leadership, rarely have anyone at the helm who understands the central importance of a shared professional identity. Foundations, therefore, tend to balkanize into feuding camps among their component staff ideologies.

Each ideological camp has its own distinctive characteristics. The program staff, if given full rein, thrive in an atmosphere of entrepreneurial ferment, where creativity is honored, innovation is rewarded, and rules are minimized. Program officers like to keep their options open, their horizons wide, and their actions unfettered. The finance staff, if given full rein, thrive in an atmosphere of honored boundaries, where following procedures is rewarded, innovation is a synonym for illicit activity, and rules are maximized. Finance workers like to keep their options delimited, their horizons within reach, and their actions trackable. Administrative staff, if given full rein, thrive best in an atmosphere of predictability, where creativity is kept within defined bounds, loyalty is rewarded, and everything operates smoothly. Administrative staff like to keep the board happy, the news positive, and their actions, like those of Caesar's wife, "above suspicion."

Clearly, there is precious little common ground to be found among these three camps. C. P. Snow's famous essay about the "two cultures" of the sciences and the humanities comes to mind here, except that foundations are even more unsettled, for there are three cultures coexisting uneasily within them.[1] The program staff and the finance staff are in a perpetual state of low-intensity conflict, for the programmer's bracing air of innovation is the accountant's noxious stench of anarchy. A great battleground of that war is met over the terms of the grants, for program officers like to give their grantees maximum creative freedom, while accountants like to limit the grantees' (as they see it) natural tendency toward transgressions by enmeshing them in a web of rules. Programmers and accountants skirmish perpetually over issues such as the conditions under which a grantee may create new line items or transfer funds among line items; whether the grant may be extended beyond its original term, and if so, for how long, and for what reason; and whether the foundation should engage in nontraditional forms of grant-making, such as challenge grants, general operating support, and (horrors) expenditure responsibility grants.

Some of these battles are over issues of fundamental importance, such as the extent to which the purpose of a grant may be altered as a project unfolds, in order to allow the grantee to react to an unforeseen problem or to seize an unexpected opportunity. Many such battles, however, are over issues of relatively middling importance, which inevitably waste the time of all involved—and sometimes get nasty. For example, I once had a grantee who made a relatively small accounting error in the first year's reporting for a promised three-year grant. An overzealous member of the accounting staff, interpreting this honest mistake as a nefarious attempt on the part of the grantee to bilk the foundation of grant funds, strenuously recommended not only that the grant be terminated but also that the foundation demand the return of the already-spent first-year funds. Sanity eventually prevailed, but the foundation's full commitment was honored only after extensive internal negotiations and intercession by the top levels of the foundation's administration.

Such conflicts do little to endear programming and accounting colleagues to each other, and it is not uncommon to hear epithets like "loose cannon" and "bean counter" bandied about. Sometimes, the tactics of war turn cruel. During the 1990s, the accounting staff at a major Midwestern foundation ruled that bottled water was not a reimbursable expense during travel in Latin America. In vain did the program staff argue that bottled water, in some parts of the world, was not a frill but rather a medical necessity. The impasse was finally broken when the program staff invited a senior accountant on a site visit to Latin America and encouraged her to partake of the local tap water. As one program officer later chuckled maliciously, this experience *moved* the finance staff to change the reimbursement rules.[2] To the administrative staff, this ongoing conflict between program officers and the accountants is an ulcer generator of the first order. Administrators, with their mantra of "Keep the board happy," witness the skirmishing with alarm and do what they can to bring peace to the organization before anyone on the board catches wind of the internal feuds. Program officers, however, perceive administrators as largely sympathetic to the accountants, for the creative process is fraught with messiness and risk, and it perpetually carries the potential of roiling the board members should something untoward occur. Program officers, therefore, feel outnumbered and oppressed by what they see as the unholy alliance between the accountants and the administrators.

This slow boil of staff tensions provides one of the reasons for scholars of philanthropy to look askance upon the entire concept of field improvement in foundations. Peter Frumkin, for example, writes of his "concern about the creeping professionalization of giving,"[3] in part because of the tendency of foundation staffs to become consumed with process, turf battles, and other purely internal concerns to the detriment of realizing a private vision of the public good. There can be no arguing the point that bureaucratic battles can get in the way of effective philanthropy. A strong case can be made, however, that professionalization is the cure for, rather than the cause of, internal infighting. A well-trained and disciplined employee is far more likely to keep focus on the foundation's mission, while a dilettante is far more likely to take aim at a colleague's real or imagined perks.

THE CEO STUCK IN THE MIDDLE, AGAIN

The stakes involved in the ideological battles among the staff, therefore, are very high and not limited to the foundation's internal affairs. The foundation's CEO, as the über-administrator, is in a highly delicate position vis-à-vis this feuding. Although he loves board-soothing good news and tranquility as much as any lower-ranking administrator, and thus would like to side with the accountants on most issues, there are usually countervailing forces that prevent him from always doing so. The most compelling of these forces is that many foundations attempt to combine the attributes of an entrepreneurial start-up organization and a mature managerial organization. If foundations were only the latter type, the CEO could afford to side with the accountants and lower-level administrators most of the time. But because many foundations are a hybrid, she must side with the program officers on several occasions.

There is, of course, a large body of literature in the field of business administration about the differences between entrepreneurial start-up organizations and mature, managerial corporations. They are very distinct creatures; the start-up is nimble, innovative, fast growing, and rule breaking, while the managerial organization is stable, steady, slow growing, and rule making. It is a given in the literature that the two different kinds of organizations require two different kinds of captains at the helm: a creative risk-taking *leader* for the entrepreneurial organization and a solid, risk-minimizing *manager* for the mature organization. The two require differing skills, differing experiences, even differing personalities, and it is rare indeed that the CEO who guided a company as a start-up can effectively continue to lead it once it grows into a mature organization.

Foundation CEOs attempting to run a hybrid organization, however, do not have the luxury of being either a leader or a manager because both their boards expect the foundation to be *both* a start-up and a mature organization at the same time. Board members (at least in theory) expect that, on the program side, foundations deliver bold, entrepreneurial innovation that will leave deep and lasting impacts upon society, while on the finance side, they deliver cautious, managerial, no-change audits. Foundation CEOs, in short, are supposed to be managing, at one and the same time, a loosey-goosey Silicon Valley–style high-tech start-up *and* a buttoned-down Wall Street securities firm.

The only way that foundation CEOs can hope to fulfill these contradictory expectations—the only way they can be both the Man of LaMancha and the Man in the Gray Flannel Suit—is to have both skill sets employed by the foundation. In their endless bickering, ironically enough, the loose cannons and the bean counters are doing only what they are supposed to do: the program officers deliver the innovation, while the accountants keep the foundation financially "above suspicion."

How, then, can this fundamental clash of cultures be resolved, particularly since each culture is essential for the healthy functioning of the self-contradictory entity that defines many modern charitable foundations? The conflict clearly cannot be resolved by consistently favoring one of the contending sides. Program officers cannot be allowed to run amok until creativity becomes indistinguishable from chaos; nor can accountants and administrators—the rule makers—be allowed to bury creativity under an avalanche of minutia. The only way to proceed is with a "both . . . and" strategy, one that tries to reconcile the irreconcilable.

The motto of foundation CEOs everywhere should be "Abandon hope of consistency, all ye who take this job." They have no alternative but to zig and zag, siding sometimes with the creatives and at other times with the rule makers, trying always to keep the two camps in a rough balance. It certainly is not easy to be both the fire and the fire brigade, but there is no other way to run a hybrid organization.

MANAGING THE HYBRID ORGANIZATION

The result, of course, is a bewildering inconsistency of thought and action, a "pushmepullyou" in which CEOs appear to be riverboat gamblers on Monday and members of the green eyeshade tribe on Tuesday, and consistency be damned, for it is impossible to keep a steady course and still deliver the contradictory results that boards and society expect of foundations. For foundation CEOs, a piece of wisdom drawn from Ralph Waldo Emerson must ever be held close to the heart: "A foolish consistency is the hobgoblin of little minds."

There may be no other way to run a hybrid organization such as a foundation, but the CEO's zigzagging is nevertheless crazy-making for a foundation's staff. Program officers feel beleaguered by accountants and administrators at all times, and when the CEO sides with them, the program officer feels like Custer at the Little Big Horn. On the other hand, when the CEO sides with the program staff, the finance staff see the camel's nose of chaos poking under the tent, and administrators fear the imminent wrath of the board. It is the CEO's task, however, to find a balance between the two camps that will allow both to thrive but neither to become dominant.

Ironically, one of the few things that bridge these gaps in ideological cohesion among the staff is their shared perception that the board is a potential threat. The program officers fear that the board will limit their creativity, the accountants fear that the audit committee of the board will object to the compromises that the CEO has forced upon them during their conflicts with the program officers, and the administrators fear that the board will become uneasy over the ferment of ideas on the staff. It is tempting for the CEO to use the staff's fears of the board as a unifying force, but if it is done at all, it should be done very judiciously. Board members rarely appreciate being cast as the bad guys in a foundation drama, no matter what beneficial effects playing such roles on occasion may have on the staff. The astute CEO will, instead, embrace inconsistency to force the various camps within the foundation to compromise.

The high road that bridges the gaps in ideological cohesion is ultimately the mission that the foundation has committed to pursue. The lofty goals found within that mission are usually the one rallying point around which all of the organization's various cultures can find a common cause. Dennis J. Prager, a distinguished practitioner of the philanthropic arts, has often admonished foundation staffs to "keep their eyes on the prize," explaining that:

> For a foundation, *The Prize* is its raison d'etre—the mission it exists to pursue, the programmatic goals it strives to attain, and the outcomes for which it holds itself accountable. Conceptually, *The Prize* drives everything a foundation does and how it does it—governance, leadership, philosophy, organizational structure, operational style, programmatic strategy, and staffing. Practically . . . *The Prize* is the banner behind which everyone marches, bringing the board, staff, grantees, and other partners together in a common, shared effort to effect a change they all agree is a worthy objective.[4]

Keeping everyone's eyes on the prize within a foundation is a matter of great urgency and great delicacy, for if the staff stray off the high road, there is always plenty of muck in which to wallow. It is perhaps understandable (but certainly not excusable), given all of the internal chaos to be managed, that foundation CEOs are so reluctant to take on additional programmatic risks. The Bard was certainly right when he penned, "Uneasy lies the head that bears the crown."

NOTES

1. C. P. Snow, *The Two Cultures and the Scientific Revolution* (Cambridge: Cambridge University Press, 1959).

2. Interview with a program officer who (understandably!) requested anonymity (29 September 2006).

3. Peter Frumkin, *Strategic Giving: The Art and Science of Philanthropy* (Chicago: University of Chicago Press, 2006), 372.

4. Dennis J. Prager, *Organizing Foundations for Maximum Impact: A Guide to Effective Philanthropy* (Washington, D.C.: Aspen Institute, 2003), 17.

THE SEVEN CHALLENGES: AFTERWORD

The seven challenges for foundation leaders do not quite equal the twelve labors that confronted Hercules, but they will require a similar mixture of wisdom and resourcefulness to overcome (although diverting a river through one's foundation is not recommended). To summarize these seven challenges in short scope, in foundations, managers inexperienced in foundation work are asked to deliver superb results from organizations staffed by people who are untrained in the field, have little in common, experience few external pressures for improvement, receive scant constructive feedback, subscribe to no common standards of good performance, and have skeptical boards and significant internal tensions. Given these burdens, given these barriers, given these bafflements, the wonder is not that there is some poor performance in the foundation world, but rather that there is so much good—even excellent—performance.

That there is so much good performance is due mainly to the fact that some foundation leaders have come to recognize the challenges for what they are and have found ways—whether systematically or by lucky guesses—to meet them. Perhaps there was a time—when foundations were few, their endowments modest, and their social impact slight—when leaving the management learning curve to chance was a sensible solution to the seven challenges. Now that foundations are many, their endowments larger, and their social impact considerable, however, there can be no good argument for relying on exceptional individual initiative or just plain good luck to teach foundation leaders how to do their jobs. The knowledge base for effective leadership exists; it need only be taken seriously by foundation boards in order to be widely taught to their staffs. It is high time that foundations are led by systematically trained and effective leaders. It is no longer enough for these critically important societal institutions to practice "random acts of kindness and senseless beauty." It is time to achieve effectiveness by design.

II

THE SEVEN DILEMMAS OF MANAGING FOUNDATIONS

8

DILEMMA I: LOW OVERHEAD VERSUS HIGH OVERHEAD

OVERHEAD SPENDING: MUCH DESPISED AND YET MUCH NEEDED

On first glance, this hardly appears to be a dilemma at all. If there is one concept that is revered in the nonprofit world, it is that of running a low-overhead organization. It has been thus since the beginning of charitable entities, and it is enshrined in the latest electronic tools, for the website Charity Navigator rates low-overhead organizations as efficiently run, while those with higher overhead are downgraded accordingly.[1] And how could it be otherwise? The less an organization spends on itself—its buildings, its administration, its staff development—the more it has to spend on those whom it intends to serve.

What seems so self-evident, however, is not completely true. Yes, it is a good idea to control overhead spending, but overhead itself is not evil; in fact, it has a number of virtues. According to the first scholarly study on the effects of nonprofit overhead, "donors and charity watchdogs often place excessive reliance on financial indicators. Of particular concern to us is the use of overhead cost and fundraising cost ratios as stand-ins for measures of program effectiveness."[2] The study's authors go on to conclude: "Yet, contrary to the popular idea that spending less in these areas is a virtue, our cases suggest that nonprofits that spend too little on infrastructure have more limited effectiveness than those that spend more reasonably."[3] In other words, a trade-off is inevitable: if overhead is kept too low, organizational effectiveness is compromised.

FOUNDATION OVERHEAD: YOU DON'T LIKE IT, BUT YOU CAN'T LIVE WITHOUT IT

What is true of nonprofit organizations in general is especially true for that distinctive type of nonprofit organization, the charitable foundation, and especially those of the private persuasion. After all, a private foundation has a fixed income, provided by its endowment. Every dollar of endowment income spent on overhead is a dollar that cannot be spent on grants. In other words, it certainly appears that every dollar of overhead *steals* a dollar from the needy and deserving grant recipients.

So where is the dilemma here? For foundations, keeping overhead as low as possible seems almost a moral imperative. When one delves deeper, however, one discovers that the truth is not at all simple; in fact, very low overhead comes at a very high price. For nonprofit organizations, the consequences of chronically low overhead have been described as "organizational anorexia." Low salaries result in constant turnover among staff. Lack of money for training employees results in lousy service to clients. The organization is undercapitalized, underfunded, and lacking essential supportive infrastructure. It limps along, as the aforementioned study has found, not nearly as effective as it could or should be. Clients, who are supposed to benefit from extremely low overhead, are actually harmed by it in the long run.

Foundations are hardly immune to the low versus high overhead trade-off. In fact, they are very susceptible, for overhead buys many of the things that we all value in foundation work. For example, one of the principal causes of the training gap discussed in chapter 1 is the obstinate refusal of foundation leaders to spend the overhead dollars needed to train their program officers. Eschewing training helps to keep overhead costs low, but it also inflicts unprepared program officers upon applicants and grantees, who pay a significant price in the form of the slipshod services they receive. Evaluation is almost universally regarded as an important and useful expenditure for foundations, for it is crucial to learn lessons today in order to improve performance tomorrow. We constantly read pundits' calls for more money to be spent on measuring the results—getting the "metrics"—of foundation projects. And yet, the more money spent on evaluation consultants, the less that is available for strictly programmatic grants. Similarly, foundations are often urged to build their grantees' organizational capacity, by funding training and technical assistance programs, and to publicize the successes of their grantees through programs of social marketing and dissemination. Some of these costs can be accounted for in the grantmaking budget, but many of them add to overhead, especially when they require more staff or outside expertise to support them.

For foundation leaders, the overhead dilemma is a problem that won't go away. Few leaders come to their positions understanding the trade-offs involved, but they soon discover them and learn that they cannot be evaded. If leaders want to attract top talent, they find that they must meet market competition in order to recruit and retain the best professionals. If leaders want program officers to serve applicants and grantees effectively, money must be spent on training programs. If leaders want to learn lessons from their grantmaking, they must hire or consult with trained evaluators. If leaders want to conduct campaigns of social marketing or dissemination, they must hire or consult with professional social marketers. Eventually, they discover that an ultra-low-overhead foundation is an ultra-unprofessional foundation, and yet, if they let overhead spending rise too high, the number and size of their grants decline accordingly.

A specific example of a foundation that was willing to embrace higher overhead in order to achieve significant impact is the Soros Foundation. During the 1980s, Soros made big bets on the playwright Vaclav Havel and his Charta 77 organization, involving trips to Prague and the eventual creation of a new Prague-based foundation to support the flowering of cultural expression and free press that had long been suppressed under communist rule. All of the travel, technical assistance, and help with communications raised the Soros Foundation's overhead expenses to a high level, but the impact that this raised level of overhead spending helped to achieve—the free and democratic nations of Slovakia and the Czech Republic—certainly justified the expenditures.[4]

FOUNDATION CRITICS: WANTING IT BOTH WAYS

Foundation leaders, who must grapple with these perplexing complexities, in most cases eventually come to terms with them. The external critics of the foundation world, however, are sometimes untroubled by complex realities. Outside pundits who promote venture philanthropy, for example, often advocate extremely high expenditures for grantee technical assistance, evaluation of funded projects, and social marketing to disseminate outcomes. Rarely do these advocates address the cost that must be paid for venture philanthropy: much higher overhead and a much smaller number of grants, since so much overhead must be spent on each grantee. Any foundation that practices venture philanthropy inevitably must become less accessible to external good ideas, for it can afford to fund only a rather exclusive group of grantees. Similarly, those critics who advocate more funding for newer, smaller, or more community-based grantees do not seem to realize that a foundation's overhead costs rise in direct proportion to the number of small grants it makes. Each grant to community-based organizations requires a good deal of investigation and due diligence, technical assistance in helping the organization meet the legal and regulatory requirements, financial processing and oversight once a commitment is made, and monitoring after the grant is in effect. All of this creates overhead, so the more small grants that are made, the more overhead erodes the grantmaking budget; ironically, this ultimately limits the amount that can be granted to newer, smaller, or more community-based organizations.

Yet, some critics of foundations either do not understand that the low versus high overhead trade-off exists or pretend that it can be evaded. Gadflies occasionally call on foundations to do more venture philanthropy or more community-based giving on the one hand, and simultaneously to hold their overhead costs to a bare minimum, on the other. Such admonitions sound persuasive to those who do not understand how foundations work, but they are just about as sensible as advising a young couple to buy an opulent mansion while simultaneously advising them to keep their monthly mortgage payments extremely low.

There is a subtler aspect of this dilemma that also must be addressed. If a private foundation CEO takes the gadflies to heart and resolves to run a truly low-overhead operation, it will mean, inevitably, that the number of its grants must be drastically curtailed. It costs just as much, after all, to cut a check for $100 as it does to cut a check for $100,000, so the fewer grants made, the lower the overhead cost. Every grant made also creates overhead in terms of due diligence prior to the award and monitoring afterward, so again, the fewer grants, the lower the overhead costs. Private foundations must make grants totaling 5 percent of their net asset value every year, so if a CEO wants to run a truly low-overhead operation, she will make the smallest possible number of big grants. Fewer grants require fewer program officers, thus containing personnel expenses. But these few large grants can hardly be made to small, emerging, or community-based organizations, for they are not large enough to absorb such huge sums. The large grants, therefore, must be made to big, established, "safe" grantees. The critics who call loudly for extremely low overhead are actually calling for a foundation that makes grants exclusively to the largest and wealthiest nonprofit organizations, such as hospitals, universities, and museums. These critics usually do not mean to advocate such a course, but if they insist upon ultra-low overhead, it leaves the foundation with very little choice.

In fact, the ultimate in low-overhead foundations would be one that made its entire annual payout requirement in a single grant to one very large (and very lucky) organization. The foundation could replace all of its programming staff with a single cash machine and operate at an unbelievably low overhead rate. This would be wonderful for the single large nonprofit organization that received all of the foundation's yearly payout in a single check, but very bad for the other 1,499,999 U.S. nonprofits that would be automatically excluded from the foundation's support.

THE POSITIVE SIDE OF FOUNDATION OVERHEAD EXPENDITURES

It needs plainly to be said that overhead buys things that everyone values and that are absolutely essential for the effective operation of foundations: due diligence so that the foundation makes the best possible social investments; financial controls so that it exercises fiduciary responsibility; monitoring so that the foundation gets the most out of its grants; evaluation so that the foundation learns lessons from its successes and failures; technical assistance so that the grantees become more effective; social marketing and dissemination so that others can emulate what works; and ultimately, professional staff, the people who make these essential functions happen. If all of these critically important elements are drastically reduced or eliminated, and foundations make a few big grants with minimal due diligence or review, the results are likely to be poor social investments, inadequate financial controls, shoddy monitoring, few lessons learned, weaker nonprofit organizations, no replication of effective programs, and incompetent foundation employees. There truly is a very high price to be paid for very low overhead.

It is, of course, possible to take a good thing too far. The *Boston Globe* investigations of 2003–2004, which discovered a handful of foundations with overhead rates so high that they made only minimal charitable grants, provides a graphic illustration of this truth. Clearly, a balance must be found between inadequate overhead on the one hand and excessive overhead on the other. Just what that happy medium of *adequate* overhead might be, however, is a moving target. A foundation operating according to the high-engagement, high-evaluation tenets of venture philanthropy will have a higher overhead percentage than one that believes in providing its grantees with generous levels of general operating support over extended periods. An overhead rate of 10 percent might be reasonable for the general operating foundation, while five times that percentage might be equally reasonable for the venture philanthropy foundation. In fact, it is not even possible to make a general statement such as, "Every foundation should keep its overhead rate below 50 percent," because operating foundations that manage their own programs routinely (and appropriately) have overhead percentages far in excess of 50 percent.

Nor is it a simple matter to calculate actual overhead rates for foundations. Current Internal Revenue Service rules allow foundations to classify as programmatic a number of costs that, to most nonaccountants, sound very much as if they should be considered as overhead expenditures. For example, the IRS allows foundations to classify portions of salaries and certain administrative costs as program-related expenses, not overhead, so if anything, true overhead rates are in actuality higher than they are reported to the IRS.

THE SILLINESS OF SIMPLISTIC SOLUTIONS

What can be said with certainty, however, is that the low overhead versus high overhead dilemma exists, and it cannot be "solved" by going to either extreme. It is good to maximize grants but bad to minimize the valuable things that overhead buys. It is good to maximize the valuable things that overhead buys but bad to minimize grants. There can be no doubt, therefore, that simplistic calls for low-overhead operation, if followed, will bring in their train a number of unintended negative consequences, including a sudden growth in the size of grants and an inevitable exclusion of all but the largest applicants from consideration. As Bruce Sievers, long a distinguished foundation executive, has noted: "Although inspired by an understandable desire to avoid expending philanthropic dollars on 'unnecessary' overhead expenses, this practice often has counter-productive results. By failing to comprehend the nature of nonprofit organizational budgeting, it can steer organizations in dysfunctional directions."[5]

The art of managing foundations, then, is among other things the art of finding the most productive balance between grant-making and grant-enriching overhead. It is a moving target, and the proper amount will vary from foundation to foundation—and even within each foundation over time. For those, however, who tout the supposed value of low-overhead operations, it is good to remember the insight of that anonymous sage who said: "For every complex problem there is a simple solution: and it is wrong."

NOTES

1. Charity Navigator, www.charitynavigator.org (22 October 2006).

2. Mark A. Hager, Thomas Pollock, Kennard Wing, and Patrick M. Rooney, "Nonprofit Overhead Cost Project: Facts and Perspectives, Brief No. 3" (Indianapolis: Center on Nonprofits and Philanthropy, Urban Institute; Center on Philanthropy, Indiana University, August 2004): 3.

3. Hager et al., "Nonprofit Overhead Cost Project," 3.

4. Joel L. Fleishman, *The Foundation: A Great American Secret: How Private Wealth Is Changing the World* (New York: PublicAffairs, 2007), 137.

5. Bruce Sievers, "Philanthropy's Blind Spots" in *Just Money: A Critique of Contemporary American Philanthropy*, ed. H. Peter Karoff (Boston: Philanthropic Initiative, 2004), 136.

9

DILEMMA 2: STRATEGIC PLANNING VERSUS FLEXIBILITY

THE COLLISION OF RIGHT AND RIGHT

As mentioned in the introduction, German historian and philosopher G. W. F. Hegel, in his study of Greek tragedy, had the insight that tragedy occurs not when right collides with wrong, but rather when right collides with right.[1] This is a perfect description of the situation in which foundations find themselves, for they receive thousands of proposals from good organizations—nonprofits in the business of health care, education, human services, arts and culture, religion, and environmental protection—and none from bad organizations such as the Ku Klux Klan. Foundations could in theory give every organization that applied an equal share of the available grant dollars. If they did, however, they would dilute their impact and inflate their overhead by making thousands of ridiculously small grants. This leaves foundations with little choice but to do that which Hegel described as tragic: selecting a few good and right proposals for funding, while turning down many more equally good and right requests.

Foundation leaders, however, rarely feel the sting of Hegelian tragedy, for they have a potent weapon in their arsenal that, as they believe, assures that only the highest and best of the proposals received are funded: the strategic plan. "In the long run," wrote Henry David Thoreau, "men hit only what they aim at." Foundation leaders, virtually across the board, would say, "Amen!" to that sentiment. In fact, strategic planning has become the closest thing to a universal article of faith in the field. For example, Dennis J. Prager states flatly that "the critical challenge facing foundations is using their resources in a focused and strategic way to identify and engage social issues with highly targeted efforts and maximum leverage."[2]

Foundations both large and small spend considerable time and resources to thoughtfully devise and implement strategic plans that will focus their grantmaking on subjects in which they have interest, experience, and expertise. Instead of dissipating resources in response to random proposals, the strategic plan concentrates the foundation's capital—both human and monetary—where it can do the most good. By so doing, strategic plans aim to assure better outcomes and magnify societal impact.

Strategic planning has been sanctified in the foundation field by both custom and theory. As early as 1913, the Reverend Frederick T. Gates, John D. Rockefeller Sr.'s philanthropic counselor, urged the oil baron to make his newly established Rockefeller Foundation an engine of "wholesale giving" and warned against the dangers of "scatteration." Rev. Gates defined this neologism as "the frittering away of too-small funds over too wide a range of charity," thus dispersing the foundation's attention into dozens of unproductive fields.[3] Only by concentrating a foundation's resources, Rev. Gates insisted, could its true potential be realized. The Rockefeller Foundation proved this point to the good Reverend's satisfaction over the following years by funding carefully planned initiatives to enormously improve medical education, including developing a vaccine to prevent yellow fever, among other great accomplishments. More recently, the proponents of venture philanthropy have stressed the crucial need to focus a foundation's plans, grants, and learning on a few essential targets if it is to make any serious social impact.

Just as with low overhead, on first blush strategic planning seems to be a blessing without a curse attached to it. And, just as with low overhead, when its soft underbelly is examined, strategic planning proves to be a great benefit that comes at a very high cost indeed; the strategic planning versus flexibility dilemma is a right versus right collision that leads a foundation inevitably to a good measure of Hegelian tragedy.

THE COSTS OF STRATEGIC PLANNING

The first cost associated with strategic planning is that of nimbleness. Although Frederick T. Gates was right to fear the dangers of scatteration, with its tendency to diffuse a foundation's impact, he should have also feared its opposite, what might be termed as *ossification* (an anonymous wit has defined the process of ossification in foundations as a disease caused by a "hardening of the categories"). In fact, Rev. Gates's colleague on the Rockefeller-funded General Education Board, Dr. Wallace Buttrick, feared ossification just as much as Gates feared scatteration. "Our one policy is to have no policy," said Dr. Buttrick. "When a thing is worth our doing, we can always find a reason."[4]

Dr. Buttrick understood that strategic planning is a process of eliminating options, which allows a foundation to aim at targets of the greatest opportunity. This process of elimination, however, also inevitably excludes any number of good and valuable targets. Are the chosen targets really better ones than those excluded through the planning process? Maybe so and maybe not, but one thing is indisputable: the very process of choosing creates limits to the foundation's range of motion. By adopting a strategic plan, the foundation has chosen a very small niche in a very large universe. If the chosen plan is to have any integrity, it is necessary for the foundation to concentrate faithfully on its execution. That act of concentration excludes literally thousands of other niches, many of which may have been just as good—or even better—choices.

Even if the foundation has chosen the perfect niche for itself, however, that happy perfection may not last for long. Strategic planning by nature is a deliberative process: it simply takes time to do it right. Usually foundations do planning while carrying on their normal workload of grantmaking, although occasionally some will make their entire year's payout in one or two large grants and then take the full year to concentrate on devising the plan. Either way, a thoughtful process takes months to complete, and it is understandable that the foundation's board, leaders, and staff become attached to it. After all of the time and money they have invested in creating the plan, they are not eager to relinquish it, or even materially to alter it, even if some better opportunity comes along. It is also the case that it takes time to devise the tactics necessary to implement the plan, sometimes as long as it took to create the plan itself. The world, however, does not unfold in synch with the stately rhythm of strategic planning. Public policy can change with the stroke of a pen; epidemics can erupt at the speed of viral replication; social movements can appear at the rate that digital information travels across the Internet. Foundations that have just completed a planning process, or that are in the middle of one, are loath to sacrifice months of such efforts to quickly respond to crises and opportunities presented by such unanticipated events. A foundation's huge investment in strategic planning quite simply robs them of their nimbleness.

THE FLEXIBLE STRATEGIC PLAN?

Foundation CEOs, especially those of the amateur persuasion, will object vociferously to the notion that strategic planning rigidifies their institutions. "Strategic plans are flexible documents," they will say. "We build 'wiggle room' into all of our planning processes so that we can rapidly adjust to changing social conditions. That way, if better opportunities or unforeseen crises come along, we can respond quickly." These CEO shibboleths are glib enough to soothe their boards, but they are also as fictitious as Harry Potter. Rarely is an unexpected crisis or opportunity so closely related to the foundation's strategic plan that a mere "adjustment" will be adequate to address it. If the foundation's strategic plan, for instance, calls for reducing the incidence of pertussis in Arizona, responding to an epidemic of avian flu in Asia is not an "adjustment" to the strategic plan, it is an abandonment of it. Moreover, when foundation employees, consultants, and board members have been focusing like a laser on developing a strategic plan for months, it is no quick and easy matter to yank them away from their considerable emotional, intellectual, financial, and even spiritual investment in this plan to turn to other topics, no matter how pressing those other topics may be. One simply cannot turn the *Queen Mary* on a dime. Amateur CEOs have been known to claim to have "solved" the strategy-flexibility trade-off by directing their program officers to spend the majority of their time on strategic issues while reserving a substantial block of their time (say a split of 75 percent to 25 percent) to be flexible and open to new opportunities and pressing problems. This sounds comprehensive when presented to trustees, but it never works in practice. No matter how bright or dedicated the program officer, it is all but impossible to be both the focused follower of the strategic plan and the flexible finder of fast-moving opportunities. Executing a strategic plan requires, above all, a focused discipline and an ability to avoid the blandishments of scatteration. Responding to crises or opportunities requires, above all, just the opposite qualities: an expansive nimbleness and an ability to avoid the blandishments of ossification. Expecting any one person to be able to function, with equal enthusiasm and ability, as an actuary and as a riverboat gambler is unrealistic to say the least, but to expect a single person to routinely toggle back and forth between these two poles on a 75 percent to 25 percent basis is utter folly.

Foundation CEOs who claim that their strategic plans have built-in flexibility are about as believable as the Soviet Union's claims that its constitution had built-in human rights for its citizens. Steven A. Schroeder, former CEO of the Robert Wood Johnson Foundation, recognized this fact when he wrote, "In my experience, a preoccupation with strategy all too often causes us to gloss over the equally important decisions about the way that a goal . . . will be implemented."[5] He went on to explain that although "foundations tend to overemphasize strategy at the expense of execution," in fact, "execution trumps strategy."[6] Schroeder is absolutely correct. Foundations tend to focus on strategic planning to the point of ossification, ironically, thus choking off the resources needed to properly execute the plan. Execution, as Schroeder says, should trump strategy, but many foundations "shoot their wad" in creating a brilliant strategy, only to discover that they have inadequate resources left to actually place it into action.

Another cost associated with strategic planning is that of significance. By its very nature, strategic planning delimits and reduces. As the focus gets smaller, the spotlight turns to problems that are more easily defined and solutions that can be more readily measured. There is a legitimate role, of course, for foundations to engage in such work. But foundations also have a long and honorable history of attacking the big issues, those that have complex causes, widespread impacts, and deep roots that make them stubborn to affect, much less to eradicate. Faced with the choice between helping students in a single school to improve their educational attainments and attacking an entire state's lousy educational outcomes, the strategic foundation will be drawn to the more modest project because it is easier to define, and it is especially easier to measure its outcomes and impact. "If foundations engage in strategic philanthropy to the exclusion of other approaches," writes Joel Fleishman of Duke University, and formerly of the Atlantic Philanthropies, "they will inexorably abdicate that wider role as providers of the social venture capital on which our society depends for its renewal."[7] Ironically enough, good strategy can become the enemy of great impact. Overreliance on strategy can lead to outcomes that are measurably positive but also demonstrably insignificant.

BALANCING STRATEGY AND OPPORTUNITY

Every day, foundations are presented with opportunities to do good. In their sheer proliferation, these opportunities inevitably conflict and compete with each other. It is right that foundations should adopt strategic plans to sort through this thicket of opportunity in a thoughtful way, so as to maximize the good they can do. But it is also right that foundations preserve the flexibility required to respond to crises and opportunities in a world that is changing at the speed of thought. In this collision of right and right, foundation leaders discover that without strategy, foundations would drown in scatteration, while without flexibility, foundations would suffocate from ossification.

Just as there is no single way to resolve the low versus high overhead dilemma, so there is no single way to resolve the strategy versus flexibility trade-off. There are, however, some important lessons. Once again, the extremes—all strategy or all flexibility—are not a legitimate answer. Nor will the wise foundation CEO pretend that all staffers can simultaneously be both focused strategic planners and nimble opportunistic grantmakers. It would be wise, therefore, to have both kinds of grantmakers on the staff. It makes sense, as well, for the CEO to assure that both kinds of grantmaking—strategic and flexible—are valued and rewarded at an appropriate level. Reward structures must be devised and allocations apportioned so that both types of grantmaker will know that it is not career suicide to work in their particular area of specialty.

The most important consideration, however, is that mentioned by Steven Schroeder, mainly that execution trumps strategy. Foundations sometimes fall into the trap of rigidly implementing a strategy that badly needs adjustment in order to work in the real world. Even the best strategies depend for their success on the quality of the tactics necessary to execute them, and sometimes these tactics must be improvised on the fly. In fact, often the only way to honor the spirit of the strategy is to dramatically alter the tactics required to implement it.

The ultimate lesson for foundation CEOs, however, is this: the notion that strategic planning is a blessing without an attendant curse is just as destructive as it is seductive. Strategic planning *is* a blessing, but like other blessings, such as wonder drugs, it confers benefits only if used in sensible moderation. If taken in too great a dose, the result is not heroic clarity but rather Hegelian tragedy.

NOTES

1. Georg Wilhelm Friedrich Hegel, *Aesthetik*, www.Britannica .com/eb/article-51139/tragedy#504976.hook (22 October 2006).

2. Dennis J. Prager, *Organizing Foundations for Maximum Impact: A Guide to Effective Philanthropy* (Washington, D.C.: Aspen Institute, 2003), 6.

3. "The Good Man," *Time Magazine* (24 September, 1956): 7, time-proxy.yaga.com/time/magazine/printout/0,8816,867100,00.html (28 November 2006).

4. Abraham Flexner, *I Remember: The Autobiography of Abraham Flexner* (New York: Simon and Schuster, 1940), 217.

5. Steven A. Schroeder, "When Execution Trumps Strategy" in *Just Money: A Critique of Contemporary American Philanthropy*, ed. H. Peter Karoff (Boston: Philanthropic Initiative, 2004), 184.

6. Schroeder, "When Execution Trumps Strategy," 184–85.

7. Joel L. Fleishman, "Simply Doing Good or Doing Good Well: Stewardship, Hubris, and Foundation Governance" in *Just Money: A Critique of Contemporary American Philanthropy*, ed. H. Peter Karoff (Boston: Philanthropic Initiative, 2004), 106.

(10)

DILEMMA 3: BROAD VERSUS DEEP

"SCATTERATE" OR CONCENTRATE

In chapter 3, mention was made of the incredible freedom that foundations enjoy: freedom from the tyranny alike of markets, electorates, and fund-raising. One tremendously important aspect of this freedom is an almost total liberty to choose the scope of a foundation's programming interests. Foundations must support organizations that meet the requirements of the relevant sections of the Internal Revenue Code, but within this universe of 1.5 million organizations, they can customize their giving at will. This seemingly limitless freedom to choose, however, bumps into a natural limit that defines the third dilemma: that of broad versus deep. Any foundation would be proud to know that it is materially contributing to the suppression of a wide range of human ills: the philanthropic equivalent of a broad-spectrum antibiotic. Any foundation would also be proud to focus on a single troublesome issue and contribute to solving it once and for all: the philanthropic equivalent of a single-disease vaccine. The trouble is, the more a foundation moves in one direction, the less it can do in the other, and ultimately if it tries to do both in equal measure, it will discover that it does neither well. Again, Hegelian tragedy is in operation. It is right to attempt to treat a broad range of human diseases. It is also right to focus on finding a cure to a single disease. Although the subject matters are similar, the two approaches are very different, for one requires a very broad gauge, across many diseases, with outcomes notoriously hard to measure (how do you count how many people did *not* die?), while the other requires a very deep approach within a single disease, with ultimate outcomes easier to measure: either a cure was discovered, or it was not. The same issues are found in other choices foundations must make. Should they try to solve the educational problems across an entire big city school system, or should they focus on improving a single school within it? Shall they try to help youth countywide, or should they concentrate on youth living in a single township?

This broad versus deep trade-off forces foundation leaders to make excruciatingly difficult decisions. If they discipline themselves and their employees to work on a single high-priority programming area, they will be forced to turn down hundreds, if not thousands, of unsolicited requests that show enormous promise. If, on the other hand, they open the foundation's doors to the wonderful ideas bubbling up from the field, they will support a number of successful programs, but Rev. Frederick Gates's scatteration will set in, and none of the programs will be supported with enough resources to create deep and lasting impact. So the choice leaders face is profound impact in a narrow range, at the cost of declining countless worthwhile requests (a mile deep and an inch wide), or shallow impact over a wide range, at the cost of superficial results (an inch deep and a mile wide).

In some cases, leaders are spared this trade-off due to the size of the foundation's corpus. A very small foundation, for example, might lack the specialized staff needed to take the lead on deep programming and end up programming broadly as a result. The

CEOs of larger foundations, however, cannot escape the dilemma. This is particularly the case when they have boards of trustees that want to have it both ways. One foundation CEO of my acquaintance recalls his exasperation at discovering that his board was about evenly divided between trustees who wanted the foundation to go deep in its programming and those who wanted it to program broadly. The mixed messages he received were maddening, especially when one of the board champions of deep programming complained about a request from one of his pet organizations that had been declined. Indeed it had—because it did not align with the highly focused programming plan that he had forcefully and consistently advocated![1]

THE MARVELS OF THE MATRIX

This CEO, bowing to the reality of his board's divided nature, adopted a management tool that purported to resolve the broad versus deep dilemma: the matrix system. Matrix systems have long been popular in business as a means of breaking down vertical "silos" by requiring employees to work across departmental lines. Essentially, the matrix is a grid on which the staff's main duties are listed along the horizontal axis, and secondary duties are listed along the vertical axis. Those duties along the horizontal axis are the "silos" in which the employee usually works, while the duties on the vertical axis cut across the silos. These crosscutting tasks, added to employees' responsibilities, are designed to break down barriers, force staff interaction, and make the entire organization into a unit. The magic, say the system's supporters, is definitely in the matrix.

The jury is still out on just how magical matrix systems are in the corporate world, but their prestidigitations have not worked particularly well in the foundation field. Just as some foundation CEOs pretend that their program officers can be both highly strategic and highly flexible at the same time, the matrix system allows CEOs to pretend that their program officers can work broadly and deeply at the same time. The system, according to its boosters, will allow the program officer to specialize ("drill deep," in foundationese) and simultaneously to do generalized crosscutting work ("go wide," in foundationese). The magic of the matrix, they would say, has solved the broad versus deep trade-off.

These matrices look great to foundation boards, for they seem to offer specialization and generalization in one handy package, thereby keeping all board members happy. No longer will there be narrow specialists, trapped in their individual silos, nor woolyheaded generalists, who are all over the programming map. No, the matrix promised a new breed of "specialized generalists" who would make the broad foundation deep and the deep foundation broad. The matrix was, in short, everybody's everything.

Alas, in every case in which such a wondrous matrix was implemented in foundations, the broad versus deep dilemma, far from being eradicated, was proven as persistent as ever. The focus, discipline, and arcane expertise required to drill deep did not translate well into efforts that required broad breadth of knowledge, a roving curiosity, and wide-ranging experience, and vice versa. Asking a grantmaker who specializes in finding ways to stimulate the construction of affordable housing for the chronically mentally ill to fund a blue-ribbon panel of wealthy citizens to plan a community-wide fine arts festival is very much like asking a neurosurgeon to diagnose a wide range of ailments in a storefront medical clinic. Time and again, the specialists floundered when asked to make the myriad connections needed to work broadly, and the generalists floundered when asked to do the highly specialized work required to drill deep. It is not that one set of skills is intrinsically better than the other; it is that they are very different skills, and the trade-off between them cannot be wished away by the creation of the matrix system, however magical it may have appeared on its surface.

(STAFF) SEGREGATION FOREVER?

Philanthropic flops though they were, matrix systems had attempted to address a real problem, that of staff segregation. Program officers who drill deep are understandably fixated on their "smokestack" to the exclusion of all other work. They tend to become uninterested in foundation-wide responsibilities, and they do not see partnership with nonspecialist colleagues as a priority. Program officers who go wide, on the other hand, understandably perceive connections everywhere. They tend to become aficionados of process (because everything connects to everything), and for that reason, they serve on numerous foundation-wide committees and community boards. They value camaraderie with their colleagues. These two tendencies make staff segregation virtually an inevitability. To the specialists, the generalists can seem jacks-of-all-trades, doing work that requires no great expertise but that does involve a suspicious amount of hale-fellow-well-met backslapping. Their programmatic work lacks rigor and has fuzzy outcomes, and most of all, they spend inordinate amounts of time in blah-blah-blah meetings. To the generalist, the specialists can seem narrowly trained and even narrower-minded people, doing work of value mainly to folks like themselves. Their programmatic activities may interest other experts, but they have little impact upon the lives of people. Most of all, specialists are free riders who care little and do less for the greater good of the foundation, the foundation field, and the wider communities that the foundation serves.

There is one more shadow on this landscape, and that is the generalists' belief that the foundation's board and executive leadership value the work of the specialist far more than that of the generalist. More often than not, this suspicion has some merit. Indeed, given society's strong bias toward specialization over generalization, it could hardly be otherwise. Specialists generally command higher salaries than generalists in most professions, so foundation leaders usually find it necessary to pay them more than generalists to work at a foundation. The work of specialists, because of its delimited, often technical nature, is usually easier to comprehend and its outcomes easier to measure than the ambitious, broadly based adaptive work done by generalists.[2] Adaptive work often results in incremental changes spread over multiple organizations or even multiple sectors of society (for instance, if thou sands of college students are inspired by foundation-funded programs to volunteer in hundreds of organizations spanning all six subsectors of nonprofit organizations, the grant has important outcomes that are so diffused that they are not easy to measure, or even to notice). When generalists reflect that their work gets less attention than that of the specialists, and that their pay is lower, even though they have the same job title, they cannot help but feel like second-class citizens within their own foundations.

The broad versus deep dilemma, therefore, operates on two levels. On one level, it presents foundation leaders with a greater than usual opportunity to maximize the performance of their program staff; on another level, it presents them with an ongoing personnel problem. Few foundations have the almost fanatical discipline it requires to choose one or two narrow areas and plunge deeply into them, to the exclusion of any and all other opportunities. But many foundations cannot resist the allure of becoming known for at least one "signature project," one programming area that requires deeply specialized expertise. Even if foundation leaders do not see such concentration as a priority, pressure to specialize will often come from program officers, who seek the prestige (and the higher pay) that comes from drilling deep on a high-status program. Thus, hybrid deep/broad foundations are quite common in the field.

A PLAN FOR INTEGRATION

The minute they drill deep, however, foundations are susceptible to the problem of staff segregation. The matrix system was
an honorable, if deeply flawed, attempt to deal with this problem, but it was doomed to failure because it addressed the
trade-off only on paper. Although the trade-off cannot be
"solved," its effects can be managed. CEOs must take the lead
in making hybrid foundations more balanced. Just as it is important to find a happy medium between the extremes of
strategic and flexible grantmaking, so it is crucial to bring broad
and deep approaches to a level of "prestige parity." The expertise needed to drill deep is significant, but it has a narrowing effect. The expertise needed to go wide is profound, yet it has a
scattering effect. These are not only different kinds of expertise
but also, and more important, *complementary* kinds of expertise. The experts need the breadth offered by the generalist, and
the generalists need the depth provided by the experts.

CEOs can bring the two together, not with the chimerical
make-work of the matrix system, but rather with a plan that raises
the status of the generalist and enhances communication between the two camps. The first objective can be partially
achieved through raising the generalists' salaries, but even more
importantly, by increasing the psychic income that the generalists
enjoy. Until they are valued more in ways both tangible and in-
tangible, no dialogue with a specialist is likely to be productive.
Then comes the task of enhancing internal communications.
There are many approaches to doing this, but one of the most
effective is to encourage the specialist and the generalist to work
together on projects of real importance. One effective method is
to create cross-group task forces that will be disbanded once the
task is completed. The task forces will not require specialists or
generalists to give up their regular work, or to "change their
spots." It will simply force them to work together for the common

good and in the process discover their complementary abilities. Given the long gestation period of the conflicts between the specialists and the generalists, these efforts will not bring about an immediate rapprochement between the two camps. But such approaches will be an essential first step in the process of correcting the problem of staff segregation.

Broad versus deep presents a straightforward dilemma but also offers a deeper implication. Since so many foundations choose to be hybrids of broad and deep, they need to understand that the two kinds of employees needed to do this—the generalists and the specialists—are alike in job title only. They will not tend to work together by natural inclination. The only way to promote productive cooperation between the broad and the deep in foundations is to find high-value work for the generalist and the specialist to do together. How many task forces and the extent of their tasks are questions that can be answered only within the individual foundations. We do know, though, that matrix systems are not the answer. The matrix, by itself, simply has no magic to bridge the chasm between the generalist and the specialist. But, although there is no simple solution that can reconcile this dilemma, there is a way to start the dialogue that will begin to minimize it. For most foundations, asking whether they should give up specialization or generalization is like asking an airplane pilot which wing, the left or the right, is expendable. The answer is that both are essential, and thus it is necessary to find a way to help both work together smoothly.

Whether the leaders' choice tends toward broad, deep, or hybrid, however, one piece of humility should be taken to heart by all foundation leaders. Abraham Flexner, an iconic program officer for the Carnegie Foundation for the Advancement of Teaching and the General Education Board during the first quarter of the twentieth century, gave sage advice in 1936 to the newly selected CEO of the Rockefeller Foundation. Flexner cautioned that America's democratic society is "envious of large fortunes and of large privately directed enterprises. There are therefore . . . limits to what a foundation may wisely attempt."[3] A healthy respect for those limits provides a giant stride toward finding the proper balance of broad and deep for any foundation, anywhere.

NOTES

1. Interview with a foundation chief executive officer who requested anonymity, 22 October 2006.

2. Ronald A. Heifetz, John V. Kania, and Mark R. Kramer, "Leading Boldly: Foundations Can Move Past Traditional Approaches to Create Social Change through Imaginative—and Even Controversial—Leadership." *Stanford Social Innovation Review* 3 (Winter 2004), 21–31.

3. Steven C. Wheatley, "The 'Natural History' of Philanthropic Management" in *Center for the Study of Philanthropy Working Papers* (Indianapolis: Center on Philanthropy, Indiana University, 1989), 12.

DILEMMA 4:
INNOVATION VERSUS IMPLEMENTATION

U.S. FOUNDATIONS: THE HOLY ROMAN EMPIRE?

There are few tasks more thankless than that of attempting to make a generalization about the programming of United States foundations, and by extension, about the skills these programs require of their employees. Some foundations are all about finding and launching the "next big thing," without much interest or concern about what happens to the idea after they help launch it. Other foundations are all about carefully nurturing funded projects until they grow to healthy maturity. Most foundations are, to some degree, in the middle—some would say the muddle—between these two extremes. They both provide the seed funds that allow new ideas to be tested and try to help guide the growth and development of these ideas.

A foundation's orientation toward funding—whether it focuses on innovation or implementation, or some hybrid of the two—dictates the kind of skills required of the foundation's program officers. A foundation targeting innovation will require people who are adept at spotting talent, who are comfortable in taking risks, and who have an entrepreneurial bent in the social sector. A foundation focusing on implementation will require people who are adept at coaching their grantees, who understand processes of organizational development, and who can provide necessary technical assistance as their grantee's organization evolves. Foundations that seek to both innovate and implement will ideally require people who are blessed with both sets of skills.

This dilemma between the urge to innovate on the one hand and the yen to implement on the other has a venerable pedigree in the foundation world. Throughout most of the twentieth century, though, the innovators had the upper hand. As recently as the mid-1960s, Warren Weaver of the Rockefeller Foundation stated flatly that the best program officers "are recruited from academic circles."[1] In other words, Weaver conceived the foundation's role as that of a midwife, helping to deliver great new ideas into the world. Management of the funded project could be largely delegated to the grantee's project director.

During all of these years, however, a steady drumbeat of voices—always in the minority, but always audible—maintained that foundations should be run "just like a business," and that, of course, required the active management of funded projects. In 1997, this argument was taken to a new level by the publication, in the *Harvard Business Review*, of an article called "Virtuous Capital," which advised foundations to mimic the organization of for-profit venture capital firms. Program officers should carefully choose projects on the basis of their potential social impacts, energetically assist in the management of those projects so as to maximize the bang realized for the foundation's buck, then plan to exit cleanly from involvement with them after they had taken off. The authors of the article even commended the venture capitalists' practice of taking a seat on the grantee's board of trustees so as to maximize the chances for success by taking a leading role in the grantee's governance.[2]

Despite the long history of bias toward innovation, and on the one hand, despite the considerable influence of the "Virtuous Capital" article on the other most foundation leaders did not see their organizations as pure bastions of innovation or as exclusive citadels of implementation. In their view, foundations—and therefore program officers—had to do both. On the front end, they had to be able to spot the talent, back the ideas, and launch the project, while on the back end, they needed to coach the project director, deal with problems, and exploit opportunities for growth. What they wanted was program officers who were both social entrepreneurs and seasoned project managers. Many foundation CEOs, as discussed in the previous chapter, found the temptation to organize by matrix irresistible, encouraging program officers to become fifty-fifty hybrids of the innovator and implementer styles, which would result (or so they hoped) in the best of both worlds: the gutsy, intuitive, decisive traits of the innovator, in combination with the thoughtful, disciplined habits of the implementer, all melding to deliver entrepreneurialism with substance and outcomes with impact.

As usual, though, there is a dilemma lurking at the core of this seemingly happy compromise. People are rarely blessed in equal measure with the heart of an entrepreneur and the soul of a manager. Most program officers feel more comfortable as one or the other, but not equally at home doing both. Moreover, in most private foundations, the tyranny of the 5 percent payout rule inevitably shifts the focus toward innovation, for the due diligence necessary to make grants responsibly tends to take time away from the oversight of funded projects. There is no comparable "5 percent management rule" to place emphasis on implementation once the grant is made. So, whether by choice or by external pressure, a majority of program officers tend to spend more time and energy developing than managing.

The two tasks are not wholly incompatible, but toggling back and forth between them (even if the program officer has the skills to do both) is certainly not an easy matter. Foundations that try to balance innovation and implementation through a fifty-fifty hybrid approach tend to turn out very much like the Holy Roman Empire, which, as waggish historians are wont to say, was neither holy nor Roman nor an empire. Such foundations, in striving for an equal balance, often end up neither innovative, nor good implementers, nor an effective combination of the two.

ENTREPRENEURS OR MANAGERS?

If a fifty-fifty hybrid style is just another fantasy of the amateur foundation CEO, the next question is whether a more sophisticated blend of innovation and implementation will work for foundations, or if they should concentrate exclusively on doing one or the other. Many grantees hold that foundations are besotted with the idea of innovation but not notably effective at actually supporting it. Far more effective, say these critics, would be the provision of general operating support for existing grantee initiatives that are chronically short of funds. Most foundation CEOs would respond that if foundations do not supply social venture capital for the new, the untried, and the experimental, just what organization or individual in society will? And, given the fact that foundations usually provide only slightly more than 2 percent of all nonprofit organization income in any given year, there simply is not enough foundation money to provide adequate operating support for nonprofit organizations.[3]

If the foundation's role as innovator is unsettled, its role as an implementer is downright controversial. Bruce Sievers, long a distinguished CEO in the foundation field, in his article unambiguously titled "If Pigs Had Wings," was among the first to question the implementation ideal as set forth in "Virtuous Capital." Sievers pointed out that the venture capital model was problematic when transferred into the world of philanthropy, especially in the level of control that it required foundations to exert over their grantees. It was by no means clear that most program officers were qualified to directly manage their grantees, but it was very clear that few nonprofit leaders would be willing to surrender their independence by allowing their funders to take seats on their boards of trustees.[4]

All of the arguments for innovation and for implementation, both pro and con, have some merit. Program officers are often not as good at either one as they think they are. But a few stark facts make it virtually inevitable that most program officers, regardless of their level of skill, will need to attempt both. First, relatively few foundations are willing to exclusively provide general operating support to nonprofit organizations, so funding innovative projects will be a large part of most program officers' grant portfolios. Second, although it might be ideal to have a program officer skilled in innovation fund the project, and then have it managed by a program officer who is skilled in implementation, this is a level of specialization in personnel that only the largest foundations could afford, and even for these megafoundations, the monies spent on hiring extra "specialist" program officers would raise overhead and reduce funds available for grants. Third, many developing projects need more technical assistance than either they can afford or the foundation can afford to provide them, so the program officer will, from time to time, be forced to pitch in. The key question, therefore, is how to avoid becoming a latter-day version of the Holy Roman Empire, neither innovative, nor good implementers, nor an effective hybrid of the two.

The answer is that this dilemma cannot be resolved, but it is possible to manage it. Four rules must be followed in order to find the right balance of innovation and implementation for an individual foundation and its program staff. These rules have to be applied with both sensitivity and flexibility, but they do provide some sign posts to help negotiate a very twisting road.

THE FOUR RULES FOR MANAGING THE INNOVATION-IMPLEMENTATION DILEMMA

The first rule is to avoid the temptation to "solve" the trade-off between innovation and implementation by requiring a program officer to be an innovator half of the time and an implementer the other half. The amount of time that individual program officers spend doing innovation or implementation is less important than the quality of the service given, and the proportions will inevitably vary from one person to the next. There are foundations in which every program officer spends more time on innovation than on implementation. Then again, one program officer might become the staff expert on implementation, so he becomes the "go-to" person for managing funded projects. The important thing is to accomplish the foundation's mission, not to arbitrarily balance the time each program officer spends innovating or implementing.

The second rule is that gaps must be filled. Invariably, not every program officer on staff possesses all of the skills needed to innovate and to implement. They may lack the tools needed to recognize promising ideas, or to connect with high-potential grantees, or to help applicants strengthen proposals so that they become fundable. Conversely, they may lack the ability to recognize a grantee's stage of organizational development, to spot a potential violation of laws or regulations governing nonprofit organizations, or to analyze a grantee's balance sheet. All of these are learnable skills, and if the foundation expects its program officers to operate effectively on both sides of this dilemma, then it needs to support training to fill these deficits. As mentioned in chapter 1, there are places to turn, such as The Grantmaking School, or resources on the Grantmakers for Effective Organizations website—and it is imperative that foundations require their program officers to take advantage of these opportunities. If all the foundation offers grantees is well-meaning but ill-trained program officers, it is doing its grantees harm.

The third rule is that the foundation must listen carefully to applicants and grantees alike to ensure that its program officers truly are fostering innovation and assisting with implementation. Far more damage has been caused in the foundation world in the name of helpfulness than in the name of malice. Applicants and grantees feel pressured to accept the help offered by program officers, even if in reality it is not at all helpful. Foundation leaders must make strenuous efforts to seek out candid responses; fortunately, the Center for Effective Philanthropy's Applicant Perception and Grantee Perception Reports, as mentioned in chapter 4, provide a practical way to get the unadulterated feedback that leaders need to assure that their program officers truly are assisting innovation and implementation, not obstructing it.

The fourth rule is that if a foundation requires its program officers to be both innovators and implementers, then it must take care to reward them appropriately for practicing both. This may sound obvious, but it is not uncommon to encounter foundation leaders who "haven't gotten the memo." I once served as a consultant to a foundation with a problem: "Every one of our program officers wants to be a lone wolf entrepreneur," said the exasperated CEO, "but no one wants to do the heavy lifting of managing our funded projects." This hardly proved a mystery worthy of Miss Marple, for a few interviews with the program staff revealed that their "obstinate" refusal to implement was actually very rational behavior. It seemed that all of the verbal kudos, big raises, and staff promotions went to program officers who were better at innovating than at implementing. This reflected a deep-seated, if unconscious, bias on the part of the foundation's leadership that valued entrepreneurs over managers, and once that pattern became clear to program officers, so did the logical response to it. The behavior that is rewarded is the behavior that management will get, and if foundation leaders regard both innovation and implementation as important, they need to tangibly (and intangibly) encourage programs officers to do both.

EXAMPLES OF SUCCESSFUL HYBRIDS

If these four rules are followed, it will be possible to manage the innovation-implementation dilemma. One example is provided by the W. K. Kellogg Foundation, which has created a "Skunk Works" modeled on the legendary design studio of the Lockheed Company, which produced such revolutionary jets as the SR-71 Blackbird and the Stealth fighters and bombers. The Skunk Works focuses on innovation, while the rest of the foundation's program staff pursue an agenda that blends innovation and implementation, with a bias toward managing projects for maximum impact. Policies are in place to encourage the rest of the program staff to adopt the innovations developed by the Skunk Works and to help with their implementation.

The Laidlaw Foundation is an example of a smaller foundation that has successfully negotiated the dilemma, by employing both innovative individual program officers and an implementing team structure. The individuals and the teams are encouraged to share proposals with each other, and the board uses a matching fund to offer incentives for joint funding of projects by individuals and teams.[5]

Smaller foundations, of course, have a more difficult time using such hybrid solutions, and if there are fewer than three program officers on staff, it becomes literally impossible to do so. In such cases, a choice must be made to be a purely innovative organization or a purely implementing organization, or to have program officers wear both hats. Any of these decisions can be the right one, as long as the foundation is consistent in practicing its choice. If, however, the choice is to be a hybrid organization, the four rules must be followed, or the foundation risks becoming a latter-day Holy Roman Empire.

THE DIFFICULTY OF GIVING IN THE RIGHT WAY

This dilemma is yet another example of how maddening it can be to effectively manage a charitable foundation. The freedom to innovate and the discipline to implement are both highly desirable and yet often incompatible. Foundation leaders frequently find themselves presiding over either a ferment of ideas that do not get realized or a smooth-functioning machine that systematically turns out mediocre work, or if they try to effect a fifty-fifty hybrid of the two, a foundation that generates bad ideas and implements them poorly. Should the foundation be large enough, the Skunk Works approach and the Laidlaw incentive program can be highly effective, but even small foundations that must choose only one style can do well if they stick consistently with their choice and cheerfully let go of what must be traded off in exchange.

Such considerations can—and should—daunt foundation CEOs and boards. Organizing a staff in the optimum manner is a difficult task, and keeping it working effectively is an ongoing challenge. It was with these pitfalls and paradoxes in mind that Dennis Prager, a distinguished practitioner in the field, observed that "giving away money *is* easy. But giving away money in the *right* way is very, very difficult."[6]

NOTES

1. Warren Weaver, *U.S. Philanthropic Foundations: Their History, Structure, Management, and Record* (New York: Harper and Row, 1967), 108.

2. Christine Letts, William Ryan, and Allen Grossman, "Virtuous Capital: What Foundations Can Learn from Venture Capitalists," *Harvard Business Review* (March/April 1997): 36–44.

3. Kim Klein, *Fundraising for Social Change* (San Francisco: Jossey-Bass, 2001), 6–7.

4. Bruce Sievers, "If Pigs Had Wings," *Foundation News and Commentary*, 38, no. 6 (November/December 1997): 44–45.

5. Nathan Gilbert, "Program Officer Team Approach," *GEOlist* (Grantmakers for Effective Organizations), www.geofunders.org/index .cfm?fuseaction=page.viewPage&PageID=454 (22 November 2006),

6. Dennis J. Prager, *Organizing Foundations for Maximum Impact: A Guide to Effective Philanthropy* (Washington, D.C.: Aspen Institute, 2003), 5.

(12)

DILEMMA 5: EXPERT BASED VERSUS COMMUNITY BASED

FILLING FOUNDATION KNOWLEDGE GAPS

Poet Robert Browning memorably wrote that "a man's reach should exceed his grasp," and that single line is a pretty fair description of a foundation's—just about any foundation's—relationship with its grantmaking. Unless it is very tightly focused on a single concentrated programming area, chances are that a foundation funds a number of areas that cross the lines of many different subjects and disciplines. The probability that its staff possesses all the knowledge needed to do effective grantmaking across this spectrum is practically nil. Outside sources of information, knowledge, and wisdom are therefore essential if a foundation wishes to develop enough grasp to empower its reach.

A knee-jerk reaction to the knowledge gaps experienced by foundations is to fill them by hiring additional staff. But this would require foundations "to take on both vast amounts of expertise and vast amounts of bureaucracy which are themselves replicating for the most part what are already being done by people who already have expertise and who already have organizations."[1] Trying to hire its way out of knowledge gaps, therefore, would swell the foundation's payroll and bloat its overhead without really solving the problem. A solution must be found that fills temporary knowledge gaps without creating permanent costs.

Over the years, foundations have developed a formidable array of advisors to whom they can turn for helpful counsel. Consultants, advisory committees, blue-ribbon commissions, task forces, and *éminences grises* all offer guidance to program officers confronting unfamiliar intellectual terrain. Much depends on the quality of advice sought and received. The literature of foundation programming is full of cautionary case studies about foundations that, for example, received inadequate counsel on programming for minority populations and made culturally inappropriate grants as a result. On a happier note, there are many cases of foundations greatly improving their programming by seeking out sound guidance before signing any checks.

The all-important question is obvious: What characterizes the best possible counselors? Clearly, the response is those who are most knowledgeable about the subject at hand. This answer, though, begs another question: Which kind of knowledge is best? There are many kinds of knowledge extant in the world, but in the realm of foundations, there are only two overarching types: knowledge learned in school and knowledge learned in the school of hard knocks. And thus arises a dilemma: for any given project, is it better to rely on expert-based knowledge or community-based knowledge? Once again, foundations confront a Hegelian tragedy in attempting to resolve this dilemma.

LEARNING VERSUS EXPERIENCE

Certainly a strong case can be made for expert knowledge. Foundation decisions should be grounded in hard data, verifiable information, and proven facts. Basing decisions on anything else—conventional wisdom, speculative approaches, old-boy networks—is at best illogical and at worst wasteful. If anyone is to be asked, does it not make sense to ask those who know the most about the subject at hand—namely, those who have researched it, debated it, and written about it? Experts understand the history of the issue, they know about projects that have been funded previously, and they have analyzed what worked about these interventions and what did not. No one could be better equipped to help shape a project with the potential to succeed where others have fallen short.

Certainly a strong case can be made for community-based knowledge as well. Foundation grants will profoundly affect a community of people, either directly or indirectly. These people should have a say in how such grants are planned and executed. In fact, H. Peter Karoff, an astute observer and promoter of the field for decades, states flatly, "Meaningful philanthropy is possible only when one listens to the voices, input and guidance of the community."[2]

This argument based on equity is supported by another argument, this one based on human nature. People tend to resent and often resist ideas that are imposed upon them without their consent. Unless they are actively represented from the very first stages of a grant program, they will not "buy in" and may respond with a range of uncooperative behaviors, from passive resistance to outright hostility. Community advice received prior to and during program implementation is, in many ways, an insurance policy against stakeholder resistance. Dennis J. Prager states the need in clear terms: "Foundations increasingly perceive that engaging key constituencies in every aspect of an initiative—from early conceptualization through the establishment of goals, priorities, and strategy development, to implementation and assessment—significantly increases the likelihood that the initiative will be developed and implemented in such a way as to be successful."[3]

To the casual observer of the foundation field, this dilemma between expert-based and community-based counsel seems to be the easiest of all the trade-offs to resolve. The straightforward solution would seem to be to seek out both experts and community leaders, then pick and choose the best advice from each to shape the grantmaking program. For a number of reasons, however, this seemingly sensible "both/and" approach is a walk through a minefield to implement.

First, the experts and the affected community almost never have any members—or ideas—in common. Anyone who has ever convened a meeting with both experts and community representatives present knows the awkwardness: on one side of the room, the experts, hailing from universities or think tanks, wearing power suits, and speaking the language of scholarship, while on the other side, the community representatives, hailing from disinvested areas, wearing T-shirts, and speaking the language of experience. The only thing that these two groups have in common, it often seems, is distrust of the other side, and community representatives are often intimidated into sullen silence by the elevated jargon and the confidently overbearing demeanor of the experts.

Second, when the two camps disagree, it falls to the program officer to mediate and ultimately to decide which course to follow. If the program officer sides with one camp too often, the other may become discouraged or even decide to boycott the process. So, in an effort to keep both camps happy, the program officer often accepts some advice from the experts, some from the community representatives, and splits the difference on other points of disagreement. The result is a program that is too community driven for the experts, too expert driven for the community representatives, and with some features that everybody actively detests. It comes as no surprise that these bastardized programs without champions to back them usually fail miserably.

Third, the experts inevitably approach the issues in a purely rational manner; they are all fact and no feeling. Community members, living in the middle of the issues as they do, have many strong emotions and are oftentimes all feeling and no fact. I learned about an example of this problem when I was responsible for a program that created new community foundations to serve isolated rural areas. In one such county, two different villages were determined to start their own separate community foundations. Experts advised that the county was too sparsely populated and had too small a resource base to support two free-standing community foundations, and they encouraged the two villages to merge their efforts. Leaders in both resisted this attempt vigorously, and in a meeting with one village's representatives, the underlying reason emerged: the other village had "stolen" the county seat designation from them "back in '57." When the foundation's representative pointed out that nearly 40 years had passed, and surely this "theft" could now be forgiven, one of the leaders responded, "No, it wasn't in 1957; it was in *1857*." None of the experts consulted had the slightest idea that this ancient grudge still had the power to affect the decisions of community leaders almost 140 years after the fact. The experts' advice, therefore, was sensible, logical, and yet completely impractical due to the level of community emotions about the history between the two towns.

Once again, the trade-off is inescapable. It is right to get advice from the greatest experts, and it is also right to get advice from the people most affected by your grantmaking. Yet, because of their differences, the more one relies on experts, the less credibility the program is likely to have in the community, while the more one relies on community representatives, the less credibility the program is likely to have with the experts. There is no completely escaping the trade-off, but is there a way to synthesize the two, perhaps not entirely, but at least enough to produce a grant program that will have some credibility in both camps?

RECONCILING ADVICE FROM THE RESEARCHERS AND THE RESIDENTS

As it happens, there is *more* than one way. Some funding programs require only one kind of expert advice, such as the medical research initiatives operated by the Howard Hughes Medical Institute. Since the issues involved are all scientific or technical, and there is no lay community directly affected, only the experts need be consulted. The great majority of all foundation programming, however, could benefit from the advice given by both the experts and community representatives. For such programs, there are better ways to get this counsel than to gather representatives of both camps in the same room at the same time. The two groups can be convened separately, with the program officer serving as the synthesizer. If this "never the twain shall meet" approach does not appeal, sometimes strictly limiting the number of advisors to one or two per camp works well; for as the number of advisors increases, so does the tendency for them to bicker (of course, limiting the number of advisors also limits how representative the sample is, an important factor to keep in mind if this route is chosen). If a joint meeting is unavoidable, it will pay huge dividends to have individual premeetings, one to train the experts on how to respect community representatives, and the other to train the community representatives on how to understand the experts' vocabulary and deal with it on a more level playing field.

A final question must be answered: Which kind of advice is to be given more weight? As previously mentioned, there are some types of grants, such as those that support esoteric research programs, that require little or no advice from community leaders. But the great majority of foundation grants will have major effects on communities, so community advice is absolutely essential, yet the programs could also benefit from the data and knowledge that only experts can provide. What is the proper balance in these cases?

The answer can be found in the old riddle about who has the greater stake in a human's breakfast, a hen or a sow? The hen surely has a stake, for she has *contributed* to that breakfast. The sow has a bigger stake, though, for she *is* that breakfast. Experts surely have a stake in a project affecting communities, for they contribute solid information and are especially valuable on the front end as the project is being conceptualized. Community representatives have a bigger stake, for they live in that community and will need to cope with the grant's impact. Their input is important from the beginning, but it becomes even more vital as the project unfolds. Anna Faith Jones, former CEO of the Boston Foundation, observes that it is "the people whose engagement and participation are most critical to successful social change. Such change cannot be imposed by politicians, or experts, or academics, or even well-intentioned persons such as those who run important philanthropic institutions."[4]

However it is done, there are some important "truth in advertising" principles that will avoid angering advisors. First, make it clear from the beginning that you will not take all of their advice: you will instead pick and choose. Second, if there are any nonnegotiable principles, you must state them up front, before soliciting their advice. Third, if experts and community leaders will be meeting separately, acknowledge the existence of one group to the other. And fourth, follow up with both camps so that they know how their advice has been incorporated into the final program.

For all of its headaches and complexities, however, the expert advice versus community advice dilemma is one with which foundation leaders must grapple. Even though the good advice from one camp will often conflict with the good advice from the other, clashing good advice is better than ill-informed action. Yes, it takes time, money, and diplomacy to synthesize the two conflicting sources of advice, but the bumper-sticker wisdom holds very true in this case: "If you think that education is expensive, try ignorance."

NOTES

1. Lisa Dropkin, Hollis A. Hope, and Vikki N. Spruill, *Making American Foundations Relevant: Conversations with 21st Century Leaders in Philanthropy* (Washington, D.C.: FoundationWorks, 2006), 13.

2. H. Peter Karoff, "Saturday Morning," in *Just Money: A Critique of Contemporary American Philanthropy*, ed. H. Peter Karoff (Boston: Philanthropic Initiative, 2004), xxii.

3. Dennis J. Prager, *Organizing Foundations for Maximum Impact: A Guide to Effective Philanthropy* (Washington, D.C.: Aspen Institute, 2003), 29.

4. Anna Faith Jones, "Doors and Mirrors," in *Just Money: A Critique of Contemporary American Philanthropy*, ed. H. Peter Karoff (Boston: Philanthropic Initiative, 2004), 58.

13

DILEMMA 6: HIGH UNCERTAINTY VERSUS LOW UNCERTAINTY

IMMORTALITY OR UNEMPLOYMENT?

All foundation CEOs dream of it: the front-page above-the-fold story in the *Chronicle of Philanthropy*, their portrait in four colors, the bold-type headline proclaiming their foundation's heroic success in eradicating one of the ancient evils afflicting humankind—disease, poverty, ignorance, warfare. All foundation CEOs dream also of this: a spacious and gracious corner office they can call their own; compensation and perquisites enough to warm the cockles of an executive's heart; and most of all, rock-solid security in their job for as long as they want to hold it. Two understandable and predictable ambitions for any CEO (to be lionized and "securitized"), but they are utterly incompatible—in other words, a trade-off. One cannot hope to be lionized without first roaming through a jungle of uncertainty and risk, while the best way to be securitized is to ruthlessly clear-cut the jungle so that risk is minimized at every turn. It is no wonder, as H. Peter Karoff notes, that the world of foundations is "a field that has historically been awash in a paradoxical mix of arrogance and insecurity."[1]

It is easy to see why foundation CEOs are tempted to achieve great things. Standing at the helm of organizations that need not answer to shareholders, electorates, or donors, that need not earn or raise money (community foundations execpted), to operate, foundations are distinctively positioned to be bold in the pursuit of great achievements. What societal organization other than a foundation would have the audacity to battle the oldest and most persistent of human problems? Enough have succeeded in grabbing the brass ring—such as the Aaron Diamond Foundation, which supported the research that largely defanged the HIV virus—to make it almost irresistible to foundation CEOs to aim at leaving behind a legacy of outsized accomplishment.

It is also easy to see why foundation CEOs are tempted to play it safe. Nearly every such CEO came to that post from another field, one in which they had to create shareholder value, or please 51 percent of an electorate, or keep peace among a posse of prickly major donors. All of these are stress-engendering, ulcer-inducing, hair-graying positions. Foundation CEOs, as the preceding chapters of this book have demonstrated, grapple with many difficulties of their own. But even the worst of these pales in comparison to the headaches involved in meeting the analysts' expectations for the next quarter, or keeping swing voters satisfied, or raising enough money to meet a payroll. As CEO jobs go, those at foundations are a pretty sweet deal. They may not command the obscenely stratospheric salaries of corporate CEOs, but they are still well compensated. They may not wield the power of a politician, but they still have clout. In fact, many foundation CEOs will tell you that the best thing about their jobs is that they no longer need to raise money. One chief executive of my acquaintance put it succinctly when she said, "If I was ever stupid enough to leave a job like this, you could make a fortune by mining the gravel from my cranium."[2] In short, it is almost irresistible to foundation CEOs to seek the high level of security that will keep them in their plum positions indefinitely.

FOUNDATION BOARDS AND THE LOVE OF CERTAINTY

Foundation CEOs are pulled in opposing directions by these two urges. Few of them got to the top of a foundation by habitually playing it safe, so most have an appetite for achievement. Their first instinct is to plunge into the roiling waters of uncertainty and follow architect Daniel Hudson Burnham's admonition to "make no small plans." This bias toward action, however, soon runs into other biases, namely those of the foundation's board. Big, daring plans create uncertainty at a very high level. Any number of nasty surprises can materialize out of that uncertainty, including broadsides on editorial pages, vituperation from bloggers, criticism from interests vested in the current dysfunctional ways of doing things, and the ever-present sniping from foundation scholars and gadflies. Board members, who tend to prize placidity above all other things, habitually frown upon such unwelcome attention. CEOs soon learn that rocking the boat will only make their board members seasick.

The high uncertainty required to achieve great things rubs the foundation's board the wrong way in another respect, as well: the potential for fallout in the political arena. The Ford Foundation has over the years been the poster child for operating under circumstances of very high uncertainty. This gutsy performance has earned the foundation a number of celebrated successes, such as the "Gray Areas" program that served as the template for Lyndon Johnson's Great Society programs, initiatives that have reformed academic disciplines, and grants that have promoted democracy in emerging nations. There were also a number of missteps, such as grants to Palestinian organizations that were later found to engage in blatantly anti-Semitic activities.[3] These generally left-of-center programs, whether successful or not, have made enemies on the right of the political spectrum, and one of them, the attorney general of the State of Michigan, filed suit in 2006, alleging that the Ford

Foundation had strayed from its donors' intentions, and attempted to force a dramatic increase in its giving to nonprofit organizations in its ancestral home, especially in the city of Detroit.[4]

Whatever the merits of the Michigan attorney general's case, there is no question but that it sent a chill down the spine of every board member in the foundation field. The suit was filed, in part, to punish a foundation that had pursued a high-uncertainty style and to warn others not to follow Ford's example. To the common genus of conflict-averse board members, this is a warning worth heeding. Any foundation CEO, therefore, who ventures far into the realm of uncertainty, is likely to encounter pushback from her nervous board. At some point, every foundation CEO realizes that there is a word to describe any of his peers whose relentless pursuit of high-uncertainty programs causes significant political fallout, and that word is *unemployed*. Conversely, no foundation CEOs have ever been fired for consistently delivering mildly successful low uncertainty in programming.

RESOLVING THE DILEMMA: TWO ACTS OF SELFLESSNESS NEEDED

Once more, this brings us to the high uncertainty versus low uncertainty dilemma. No foundation CEO wants to be remembered as "Mr. Played-It-Safe," but no one wants to be remembered as "Mr. Got-the-Gate," either. The only way to achieve great outcomes is to embrace great programmatic uncertainty, and yet the best way to keep the key to the corner office is to immunize against programmatic uncertainty. How can this trade-off be resolved?

The short answer is that there is no resolving it. If the CEO chooses a pure course of high uncertainty, she may alienate her board and lose her job before the big programmatic bets she has made have a chance to mature. If a CEO chooses a pure course of low uncertainty, he will probably keep his job indefinitely, unless enough board members realize that his outcomes are such tepid successes that his job is hardly worth doing. In order to achieve significant outcomes while keeping her job, therefore, the foundation CEO needs to find the proper mixture of certainty and uncertainty, but at what proportions?

John F. Kennedy was fond of quoting the old proverb that it is impossible to make an omelet without breaking a few eggs. Foundation CEOs must avoid the temptation to pretend that they can make that omelet of high-uncertainty programming without breaking a few eggs of certainty. In short, the only way to fulfill the foundation's potential is for its CEO to inject uncertainty into its programming, enough, in fact, to place himself into potential jeopardy. In most cases, this means that the foundation's program should have a marked bias toward high uncertainty. This does not mean that all of its programming should be on that side of the ledger, nor does it mean that it should program recklessly. This does mean that it should take calculated risks, tempered by some appropriate level of low-uncertainty programming, knowing full well that controversy and political fallout may ensue, especially if the riskier programs fail to deliver.

The classic example of a foundation leader who took very real and very large—yet very calculated—risks and won big is Irene Diamond. She had demonstrated her eye for the main chance during her years as a Hollywood producer when she shepherded the movie *Casablanca* through to production. In the late 1980s as CEO of the Aaron Diamond Foundation, named for her late husband, she made the audacious decision to focus nearly all of the foundation's giving on the creation and operation of the best HIV/AIDS research laboratory in the world. This was nothing if not a risky proposition. HIV/AIDS was then a relatively new and poorly understood virus, so the chance of the research coming to nothing was quite high. The social risks, however, were even greater, for many homophobic groups in society regarded HIV/AIDS as divine retribution for the sins of homosexuals, while gay activists, led by the protest group ACT UP, responded strongly—sometimes violently—to the neglect, benign and otherwise, that the disease and its victims were receiving. Indeed, Mrs. Diamond's first meeting on the subject was disrupted by an ACT UP protest. Clearly, there were any number of lower-risk programs that the Aaron Diamond Foundation could have supported, but its CEO calculated the risks and persevered with her support of the research of the HIV/AIDS lab. And, after a few years, Mrs. Diamond's vision and courage were vindicated when the lab produced the protease inhibitors that have made the anti-AIDS "cocktail" so effective and that have prolonged so many lives.[5] Yes, there were any number of safer routes for Irene Diamond to choose, but few that would offer so much benefit to so many—if she and her foundation were willing to work and live with high uncertainty.

Emulating Irene Diamond will require two acts of selfless leadership. First, it will require CEOs to place at risk the best job they could ever hope to have. Perhaps my friend was correct in saying that this would be evidence of having large deposits of alluvial grit where one's brain ought to be, but it is also the right thing to do. Foundations are chartered, after all, to serve the common good, not to serve as comfortable sinecures for chief executives. It will also require courageous selflessness on the part of the board members, who will have to surrender their excessive fondness for the even keel. Certainly, smooth sailing is always more pleasant than rough seas, but foundations are chartered to comfort the afflicted, and sometimes in order to fulfill that noble purpose, it becomes necessary to afflict the comfortable— namely, their comfortable trustees—with some significant unpleasantness: controversy, accusations, even, as previously mentioned, lawsuits. As H. Peter Karoff says, "In order for philanthropy to be great, to be heroic, we have to believe in ourselves and put away the Silly Putty of insecurity."[6] No reward has ever been received, after all, without first accepting some risk.

Ultimately, despite all of its comforts and its perquisites, the position of a foundation CEO is a dream job if—and only if—its power is used boldly to help make other dreams come true. The sole means of realizing these dreams, ironically enough, is to risk awakening from them. Pure low-uncertainty programming will, in the end, bring only one thing to its practitioner: the sure knowledge that he or she squandered the power and the promise of the foundation to serve society, and all for the purely selfish motive of keeping a great job. This is not the kind of eulogy one would be eager to have carved into one's tombstone.

NOTES

1. H. Peter Karoff, "Saturday Morning: A Reflection on the Golden Age of Philanthropy," in *Just Money: A Critique of Contemporary American Philanthropy*, ed. H. Peter Karoff (Boston: Philanthropic Initiative, 2004), 8.

2. Interview with a foundation CEO who requested anonymity, 9 November 2006.

3. Scott Sherman, "Target Ford," *The Nation* (5 June, 2006), www.thenation.com/doc/20060605/sherman (11 November, 2006).

4. Ian Wilhelm, "Michigan A.G. Investigates Ford Foundation, Seeks Increase in Grants for the State," *Chronicle of Philanthropy* (6 April, 2006), www.philanthropy.com/free/update/2006040601.htm (10 April, 2006).

5. Peter Frumkin, *Strategic Giving: The Art and Science of Philanthropy* (Chicago: University of Chicago Press, 2006), 132–33.

6. Karoff, "Saturday Morning," 20.

(14)

DILEMMA 7: HIGH PROFILE VERSUS LOW PROFILE

LOW PROFILE OR NO PROFILE?

"It is a riddle wrapped in a mystery inside an enigma." Sir Winston Churchill was speaking of the Soviet Union when he uttered this sentence, but he could, with equal accuracy, have been describing much of the foundation world, which actively shuns publicity of any sort. A majority of all foundations do not publish an annual report, nor do they maintain a website, nor do they employ anyone whose primary responsibility is keeping an open channel to the media or to the broader public. Joel Fleishman refers to this notoriety-shy stance as a "'culture of diffidence' that discourages openness about their activities and agendas."[1] Even among those foundations that do not hide from the press, there is considerable ambivalence: their relationship with the fourth estate is characterized by approach and avoidance in about equal measures. As mentioned in the last chapter, many a foundation CEO would dearly love to be featured, along with his foundation, in a laudatory article on the front page of the *Chronicle of Philanthropy*, but just about every such CEO lives in unholy horror of being featured, along with her foundation, in a critical article published in the same newspaper.

In short, CEOs want it both ways: when the foundation wants to tout a successful grant, they want the press to swarm around as if they were teen idols at a high school dance. Conversely, when the foundation has an embarrassing fizzle on its hands, they want the press nowhere to be seen so that the failed project can dematerialize in blessed silence. It would be handy if it were possible to get publicity on demand—to toggle back and forth between the limelight and the dark wings of the stage when needed and desired—but it simply cannot be done. Once more a dilemma is involved: the high profile versus the low profile.

Foundation boards, with their allergies to risk and their addictions to smooth sailing, are magnetically drawn to the low-profile approach. Moreover, since there is no way to achieve notoriety without enduring some hard scrutiny, the higher the profile of the foundation, the more negativity and close examination it must endure. Many foundation leaders are most comfortable, therefore, with a consistently low profile, a place comfortably (and perpetually) beneath the radar. Here, criticism never reaches the top echelons of the foundation's leadership, the skies are forever cloudless, and all is well with the world.

The low-profile foundation, however, cannot escape the high profile versus low profile trade-off. Whenever such a foundation has a big success to share with the world, leaders quickly discover that they have no contacts in the press or the media with whom to share it. Their foundation has been so quiet for so long that it is not so much a "low profile" foundation as it is a "no profile" foundation. It simply has no reputation, no friends, no real means of effectively disseminating good news. Similarly, whenever regulators attempt to impose a misguided rule upon the foundation world, its low-profile members find they are utterly unknown and unappreciated among the general public and the public's political representatives when they attempt to plead their case.

GRANTEES IN THE SPOTLIGHT

As usual, foundation leaders are ready with rationalizations for being shrinking violets. The time-honored argument for low-profile work in foundations was articulated almost as soon as foundations appeared in the United States. Andrew Carnegie, who established twenty-three different charitable foundations and trusts in his lifetime (and funded 2,509 library buildings, for good measure), strongly believed that foundations, like wealthy individuals, should "set an example of modest, unostentatious living, shunning display or extravagances."[2] Carnegie's successors in the field tended to agree. It was the grantees who did the work, they pointed out, the grantees who owned the programs, the grantees who succeeded or failed. It followed, therefore, that if it made sense to publicize the projects, it should be—indeed it *must* be—the grantees who sought and benefited from the attention.

Many foundation leaders take such logic a step further, arguing that it is not only appropriate for grantees to get the publicity, it is also a matter of good taste. A 2006 study discovered that foundations "avoid the limelight because they don't want to be perceived as braggarts or steal the thunder from grantees."[3] Foundations, this line of thinking goes, are in the business of supporting the good works done by others and should not have agendas of their own. It would be unseemly, therefore, if foundations were to muscle their way into another organization's spotlight. Any foundation that attempted to advance its own interest through publicity is more than a little gauche. No, the proper place for a foundation is in the background, quietly and effectively making grants behind the scenes and never taking a bow in public. One might even say that people should "pay no attention to the funder behind the curtain."

There is much to be said for this vision of a foundation as an empowering and enabling entity, concentrating its energies

upon helping its grantees. Many foundations over the years
have played the part of producer to their grantees' role as actors
with aplomb and discreet distinction. The Andrew W. Mellon
Foundation comes immediately to mind, with its long history of
providing major support for scholarship, such as the creation of
massive digital databases, to prestigious universities, all the
while operating effectively and unobtrusively in the background. It is a highly valuable if somewhat genteel stance, rem-
iniscent of a formal great uncle who still dresses for dinner.

Yet there is a price to pay for this retiring style, both for the
foundation itself and for the foundation field. Foundation leaders
are forever decrying the difficulty they experience in getting the
press interested in especially high-impact projects that they fund.
This is hardly surprising, however, for their reluctance to engage
with reporters under unpleasant circumstances means that they
have no relationship with them during pleasanter times. The entire foundation field pays, as well, for the general reticence to engage gives reporters little incentive to develop any expertise
about foundations. Thus, outside of the small and knowledgeable
trade press led by the *Chronicle of Philanthropy*, when a scandal
erupts, the coverage is provided by correspondents who usually
misunderstand and often garble the issues at hand. For example,
when the *Philadelphia Inquirer* ran a major investigative series
on nonprofit organizations and foundations in 1993, the lead reporters did not understand the function of endowments and ac-
cused nonprofits and foundations alike of "warehousing wealth,"
which they defined as hoarding charitable dollars instead of
spending them immediately for public benefit.[4] The reporters
simply did not understand that endowments provide perpetual
income to support the ongoing programmatic work of both nonprofit organizations and foundations.

The price that the field pays to avoid the occasional embarrassing media story is thus a huge one. Not only does the lack
of media contacts make it very difficult for foundations to dis-

seminate good outcomes and thus magnify the impact of their projects, but the failure to nurture a knowledgeable core of reporters condemns the field to be misconstrued and misunderstood in those stories that do get written. Most concerningly of all, during times of scandal or regulatory crisis, there are few independent voices in the media that can counter the errors provided by the misinformed or downright malicious critics.

BENEFITS OF EMERGING FROM THE SHELL

In recent years, some foundations have taken some proactive steps to interact with the media. A case in point is contributions made to National Public Radio and the Public Broadcasting Service, which entitle the foundations to have their taglines read over the airwaves at specified times, thus reaching these media outlets and their influential audiences with a positive message about foundation missions and activities. Inevitably, there are missteps—one foundation has used its spot to promote a book written by its CEO—but overall, this represents an encouraging outreach to important audiences who otherwise might be little acquainted with foundations or their work.

But there must be more comprehensive efforts to resolve this dilemma. Unless the field is willing to come out of its shell, however, nothing can be done. The comforts that shell offers are considerable: it shields the foundations' flubs from the prying eyes of the outside world, thus allowing CEOs to rest secure in their dream jobs and allowing board members to enjoy unruffled calm in their meetings. But the shell is also an impermeable barrier that prevents the outside world from understanding what foundations do, what they achieve, and why they are important. In times of scandal or regulatory crisis, therefore, the shell appears to be a sinister fortress that implies foundation wrongdoing simply because it prevents transparency.

Cracking the shell makes sense, but it is not without its discomforts. Everyone in foundations has grown accustomed to
quietly burying their mistakes without the need to explain or ac-
count for them. If the shell goes away and the field becomes
transparent, everyone will need to operate in the harsh light of
day and take full responsibility for their errors. CEOs will have
to surrender some job security, and board members will have to
learn to cope with informed outside criticism. There will be
moments of embarrassment, as the spotlight is trained on the
foibles of the foundation and grantee alike. There may even be
a few "deer in-the-headlights" moments until the foundation
leaders get used to living the examined life.

But the data strongly suggest that there will be only a few
such moments. The Philanthropy Awareness Initiative (PAI) examined 38,000 news stories about philanthropy and the foundation world published from 1980 to 2005, and "One finding of
the PAI media audit was that only 1% of the coverage of philanthropy over the past 15 years was negative."[5] Once more, the
field is paying a very high price in order to avoid a mere 380
negative stories spread over a period of fifteen years.

Sunlight, it is said, is the best disinfectant. There can be little
question but that replacing the shell with a new transparent
stance will cause occasional short-term discomforts but will
prove vastly beneficial in the long run. In our wired age, the old
shell is not long for this world in any case, for bloggers will systematically chip at it until it disappears. It makes sense, therefore, to proactively let the sunshine in. The short-term costs of
greater scrutiny will pay multiple long-term dividends in terms
of informed reporters; established relationships; and more accurate broadcasts, articles, blogs, and books.

Ultimately, a higher-profile stance will provide one enormous
benefit for all foundations. It will remove the perception that
any organizations that are so secretive, so retiring, and so reti-
cent must have something sinister to hide. The reputation for

transparency, once developed, will project the opposite image: a field that is confident enough to be, like Oliver Cromwell, painted "warts and all." The warts may embarrass from time to time, but a more open face will more than compensate for it. As Albert M. Sacks has noted, the "notion that philanthropy . . . must remain noncontroversial represents a fundamental misunderstanding of the institution, which not only perverts its historical development, but also destroys its essential values.[6]

NOTES

1. Joel Fleishman, *The Foundation: A Great American Secret* (New York: PublicAffairs, 2007), 156.

2. Andrew Carnegie, "The Gospel of Wealth," in *America's Voluntary Spirit: A Book of Readings*, ed. Brian O'Connell (New York: Foundation Center, 1983), 104.

3. Lisa Dropkin, Hollis A. Hope, and Vikki N. Spruill, *Making American Foundations Relevant: Conversations with 21st Century Leaders in Philanthropy* (New York: FoundationWorks, 2006), 5.

4. Editorial, "The Nonprofit Biz: Tax-Free Institutions Have Multiplied; Many Simply Aren't Worth the Cost," *Philadelphia Inquirer*, 25 April 1993.

5. Dropkin, Hope, and Spruill, *Making American Foundations Relevant*, 17.

6. Warren Weaver, *U. S. Philanthropic Foundations: Their History, Structure, Management, and Record* (New York: Harper & Row, 1967), 198.

THE SEVEN DILEMMAS: AFTERWORD

The seven dilemmas for foundation leaders truly teach us the meaning of Hegelian tragedy, for they daily force these leaders to confront decisions between right and just alternatives, making it impossible to select any good choice without rejecting one or more equally good choices. To summarize these seven dilemmas in short scope, in foundations, managers inexperienced in foundation work are asked to deliver superb results from organizations that are constantly torn between the high payout made possible by low overhead and the improved effectiveness that high overhead provides; between the need to narrow choices and the need to be open to them; between the desire to do the greatest good for the greatest number and the desire to make a profound impact in a limited scope; between the urge to create new answers to old problems and the need to prudently manage existing resources; between the advice given by experts and the advice given by those who have to live with the results; between the potentially enormous benefits offered by high uncertainty and the greatly minimized risks offered by low uncertainty; between an insecure life in the limelight and a secure life in the darkened wings. The choices are all so good that eliminating any one of them feels bad, and yet leaders cannot live in the no man's land between the choices. When right and right collide, the tragic decision must be made to choose one right over another, to do one good thing at the expense of another equally good thing.

Despite all of the freedoms that foundations enjoy—the freedom alike from the disciplines of the market, the electorate, and the fund-raiser—these dilemmas demand choices that no foundation leader can escape. Within these dilemmas, there are prices to pay, people to hurt, and causes to forsake. It is simply impossible to choose one course without eschewing others, to embrace one plan without rejecting others. As the old wisdom affirms, for every winner, there is a long line of losers.

Yet, in the midst of all of this Hegelian tragedy, there is also room for hope. When foundation leaders recognize the dilemmas for what they are, when they cease the fruitless search for silver bullet solutions, when they embrace the contradictions inherent in the dilemmas and earnestly search for "third ways" within them, then the Hegelian tragedy can be softened. The dilemmas never get "solved," never entirely go away, but at least they can be managed. This is not the same thing as having it both ways. Even when the dilemmas are well managed, hard choices still have to be made, and many good people and good organizations still must be rejected. But as long as the managers can articulate what was traded off for the choices made, and why those decisions were reached, the foundation can find a place between the dilemmas' horns. Perhaps this is the origin of the old aphorism about "taking the bull by the horns and facing the situation."

EPILOGUE

FORTY YEARS ON

Foundations have over recent years been under fire. There have been official investigations, and there has been some criticism in news media, in articles, and in books. The official investigations, and some of the private inquiries, have turned up some instances of practices which, whether or not narrowly legal, are obviously and in a very few cases, outrageously bad.[1]

If it were not for the omission of blogs from the sources of criticism outlined above, the statement could date from 2007, not as it in fact does, from precisely forty years before, from 1967. When Warren Weaver wrote these words four decades ago, foundations were under scrutiny by Representative Wright Patman, a Texas Democrat, who eventually succeeded in shepherding through Congress a sweeping overhaul of the laws regulating the field, contained within the Tax Reform Act of 1969. Despite these structural changes, however, many of the actual practices of foundations have not markedly changed during the subsequent forty years. Once again, the media, led by the *Boston Globe*, are writing critical stories. Once again, regulators—in particular Senator Charles Grassley, Republican of Iowa—have been examining the practices of foundations. Once again, foundations face the distinct possibility that a major effort to regulate their activities will be launched in Congress.

How has it come to pass that during forty years of enormous social, economic, and technological progress, during a time when foundations grew wealthier and could bring to bear so much more sophisticated technology to support their work, that foundation effectiveness (aside from a handful of exemplary institutions) has improved only marginally, if at all? Why is it that Warren Weaver's assessment sounds so fresh and contemporary today? Why does Weaver's 1967 quote that opens the last chapter of this book sound so much like Michael Porter's 2006 complaint that opened its introduction, that foundations are pissing away money on ineffective projects?[2] There are two answers to this question, one rather obvious and the other rather subtle.

JOIN THE CLUB

The obvious answer is that foundations have stubbornly resisted the tide of professionalism that has washed over most fields of practice. They have remained a desert island of amateurism in a deepening sea of standards. While other fields have defined good practices, emphasized prehire training and posthire continuing education, and created career paths that stress continuous improvement, foundations have continued to operate (as Shakespeare would have said) sans good practices, sans training, sans continuing education, sans career path, sans everything. In a world of workers who have taken their professions seriously, foundations have continued to be a dilettante's haven, resembling far more a nineteenth-century British gentlemen's club than a twenty-first-century knowledge organization.

In the absence of a fieldwide impetus to improve, the quality of practice has advanced in small, self-motivated pockets of excellence but has mostly languished everywhere else. The advent of The Grantmaking School and GrantCraft has allowed individual program officers to take their jobs seriously by elevating their level of practice. Foundations that are serious about operating in a professional manner now have a place to congregate—Grantmakers for Effective Organizations gave them a club of their own—but of the 80,000 foundations in the United States, not even 300 have joined the Grantmakers for Effective Organizations as premium (paying) members.[3] In most foundations, however, and in most areas of the country, applicants and grantees are treated no worse—but unfortunately little better—than they were treated in Warren Weaver's day. And, as Weaver's statement that opens this chapter indicates, applicants and grantees were not treated particularly well in his day. It is difficult in the extreme to imagine how organizations having the resources needed to pay for improvements in their practice can justify failing to do so.

Foundation effectiveness has also lagged for another far more subtle reason: the remarkably ahistorical nature of the foundation field. It is a very rare foundation employee, indeed, who knows even the most rudimentary facts about the field's rich heritage. The typical program officer might be vaguely aware that somebody named Andrew Carnegie wrote an article called "The Gospel of Wealth," although this officer probably has never actually read it. The other classics in the field, written by people such as Julius Rosenwald, F. Emerson Andrews, Dwight McDonald, Waldemar Nielsen, Alan Pifer, and Warren Weaver, are as remote to him as the contents of Babylonian cuneiform texts. The pathbreaking accomplishments of the Carnegie Corporation of New York, the Rockefeller Foundation, the General Education Board, and the Russell Sage Foundation might as well have taken place on one of the remoter moons of Saturn as on the third planet from the sun. As far as typical foundation employees are concerned, the history of their own foundation—indeed, the history of the entire foundation field in the United States—did not begin until the first time they walked through their own employer's front door.

This ahistorical bias has a number of practical consequences. George Santayana's celebrated observation that "those who cannot remember the past are condemned to repeat it" is rarely truer than it is in the foundation world. Foundation leaders, blissfully unaware of the lessons provided by past practice, repeatedly stumble over the very same challenges and dilemmas that felled their predecessors. This cycle of repetitious failure could be avoided by teaching the field's knowledge base to new leaders, but such trainings are the exception rather than the rule. The failure cycle's obverse—the success cycle—also is in full swing, expressing itself as an endless loop of reinvention. Every year, foundations herald a "bold new departure" in their programming that is "unprecedented in the history of philanthropy." Occasionally, one of these claims proves to actually be true. Far more often, upon examination, this "bold departure from past practice" turns out to be worthy but also unwittingly recycled from an earlier era of foundation history. The Bill and Melinda Gates Foundation, for example, has been widely praised for its major initiatives to wipe out diseases such as HIV/AIDS and malaria, with the lay press routinely describing such efforts as unexampled in their ambition and their size. In fact, as the leaders of the Gates Foundation would be the first to acknowledge, the Rockefeller Foundation wiped out yellow fever, and the General Education Board eliminated hookworm, both nearly a century before the Gates Foundation began its good work, and if Gates's current spending were to be deflated to "roaring twenties" values, the sums spent by the pioneering foundations would be quite comparable.

Every year, new foundation employees take their posts, as I did in the mid-1980s, knowing very little about the heritage of foundations but passionate in the belief that foundations of the past were plodding, stodgy creatures, badly in need of the revolutionary ideas that fresh troops like themselves have in such abundance. Those "revolutionaries" who stayed in the field long enough eventually learned, as I did, that subsequent waves of new program officers and managers perceived them exactly as they had perceived their predecessors: as hopeless dullards who needed to learn how *real* grantmaking is done. Ahistoricism thus results in a sort of intergenerational Kabuki drama, a perpetual silly cycle of wasteful repetition of mistakes and clueless reinvention of successes, all for want of a sense of history (not to mention a want of humility). Unlike Sir Isaac Newton, who believed that he could see farther by standing on the shoulders of giants, today's foundation leaders know of no giants among their predecessors, so they usually end up seeing no farther than their predecessors did.

The full absurdity of this Kabuki drama becomes evident if one imagines it transferred to other fields. Consider the chaos that would ensue if each new attorney had neither statutes nor precedents to guide her and had to create the law as she went along. Consider the lives lost needlessly if each new physician had neither case studies nor pharmaceuticals from the past and had to devise new diagnoses and treatments on the fly. Our attorney and our physician would never dream of practicing without first benefiting from the rich legacy of thought and action bequeathed to them by those who have gone before in their professions, and their practices (not to mention their clients and patients) benefit enormously from their doing so. Attorneys and physicians take Newton's advice and stand on the shoulders of giants. Why do foundation leaders see no value in standing on the shoulders of a John Gardner, an Abraham Flexner, an Alan Pifer, a Paul Ylvisaker, or more recently, an Irene Diamond or an Emmet Carson?

FOUNDATIONS SHOULD PAY (ATTENTION) TO THE PIFER

In 1984, Alan Pifer capped his distinguished career as president of the Carnegie Corporation of New York (1967–1982) by writing an essay titled "Speaking Out," in which he reflected on his thirty years in the foundation field. Pifer pulled no punches in his essay, taking his former foundation field colleagues to task for their arrogance, discourtesy, and timidity.[4] He argued that the best grantmaking is that which mixed education, especially extensive reading in numerous fields, with a passionate compassion, a mixture of the head and the heart.[5] It was this melding of intellect and emotions that made the ideal grantmaker. Pifer summed it up in a beautifully written paragraph:

> Above all other aspects of foundation work, I would put the human factor. I mean by this the attitudes and behavior of foundation staff members. If they are arrogant, self-important, dogmatic, conscious of power and status, or filled with a sense of their omniscience—traits which the stewardship of money tends to bring out in people—the foundation they serve cannot be a good one. If, on the other hand, they have a genuine humility, are conscious of their own limitations, are aware that money does not confer wisdom, are humane, intellectually alive and curious people—men and women who above all else are eager to learn from others—the foundation they serve will probably be a good one. In short, the human qualities of its staff may in the end be far more important to what a foundation accomplishes than any other considerations.[6]

The "human qualities" of which Pifer spoke are at once the glory and the disgrace of philanthropy, the wellspring of foundation success, and the source of much foundation failure. Human qualities have produced people like Alan Pifer, who strove to balance the heart and the head, and it also produced others who were

all heart or all head, or in rare cases, deficient in both depart-
ments. Foundation failure occurs not because effective philanthropy is intellectually unattainable, nor because it is emotionally
overwhelming; the challenges that must be met and the dilemmas
that must be reconciled are daunting but ultimately manageable.
The affective issues involved in effective philanthropy are sometimes wrenching but ultimately can be overcome. It is critically
important to note, however, that challenges and dilemmas cannot
be managed, nor can emotions be properly channeled, unless the
practitioner takes grantmaking *seriously*. Unfortunately, as Pifer
notes, "Some officers seem to lack the deep commitment to their
work that would lead them to make substantial investments of
their own emotional, intellectual and psychic capital in it."[7] This is
the ultimate irony of foundation failure: a field that makes $40 bil-
lion in grants annually fails to invest even a modest sum in its own
current quality and its own future vitality.

Pifer held the foundation field's feet to the fire, writing:

> I have always felt, however, that because [foundations] are such
> privileged institutions, and because they have so much potential
> for unusual service to the society, foundations should be judged
> by a higher standard. Simply behaving in a publicly inoffensive
> manner, or just staying within the limited requirements of the
> law, are hardly sufficient tests for them to meet. They should be
> measured, and should measure themselves, by much more de-
> manding standards and goals.[8]

Few would disagree with Pifer's call for foundations to hold
themselves to a higher standard of performance. Fewer still
would argue that many foundations have actually attained this
lofty plateau of performance. It has ever been thus among U.S.
foundations, but it does not mean that this fundamentally ahistorical field is inevitably a prisoner of its own past. By simple
acts of will, the foundation field can find the giants of its past,

climb upon their shoulders, identify good practices and teach them, reject the failures, and embrace what works. By taking the calling of grantmaking seriously, by choosing effectiveness over idiosyncrasy, foundations will rise in the public esteem because they will finally fulfill their high missions. This will be a great day for all United States foundations. It will be an even greater day for the people and for the societies that these foundations serve.

NOTES

1. Warren Weaver, *American Foundations: Their History, Structure, Management, and Record* (New York: Harper and Row, 1967), xiii–xiv.

2. Matthew Bishop, "The Business of Giving," *The Economist* 378, no. 8466 (February 25–March 3, 2006): 4.

3. www.geofunders.org (9 December 2006).

4. Alan J. Pifer, "Speaking Out: Reflections on 30 Years of Foundation Work," *Foundation News & Commentary* 38, no. 4 (July/August 1997), www.foundationnews.org/CME/article.cfm?ID=2377 (9 December 2006).

5. Pifer, "Speaking Out."

6. Pifer, "Speaking Out."

7. Pifer, "Speaking Out."

8. Pifer, "Speaking Out."

BIBLIOGRAPHY

Baker, Russ. "Cracks in a Foundation: The Freedom Forum Narrows Its Vision." *Columbia Journalism Review*, www.cjr.org/issues/2002/1/cracks-baker.asp? (19 September 2006).

Bishop, Matthew. "The Business of Giving." *The Economist* 378, no. 8466 (February 25–March 3, 2006): 3–5.

Bolduc, Kevin, Phil Buchanan, and Judy Huang. *What Nonprofits Value in Their Foundation Funders*. New York: Center for Effective Philanthropy, 2004.

Buchanan, Phil, Ellie Buteau, Sarah Di Troia, and Romero Hayman. *Beyond Compliance: The Trustee Viewpoint on Effective Foundation Governance: A Report on Phase II of the Center for Effective Philanthropy's Foundation Governance Project*. Boston: Center for Effective Philanthropy, 2005.

Carnegie, Andrew. "The Gospel of Wealth." In *America's Voluntary Spirit: A Book of Readings*, edited by Brian O'Connell (pp. 47–108). New York: Foundation Center, 1983.

Center for Effective Philanthropy. "Assessment Tools: Applicant Perception Report." www.effectivephilanthropy.org/assessment/assessment_apr.html (5 June 2006).

———. "Assessment Tools: Grantee Perception Report." www.effectivephilanthropy.org/assessment/assessment_gpr.html (5 June 2006).

Council on Foundations. "Principles and Practices for Effective Grant-making." www.cof.org/Learn/content.cfm?ItemNumber=776 (21 September 2006).

David, Tom. "Ready, Set, Learn: The Foundation as a Learning Organization." *Learning* (July 2006), Grantmakers for Effective Organizations.

Doyle, Sir Arthur Conan. "Silver Blaze." In *The Memoirs of Sherlock Holmes*. Oxford: Oxford University Press, 1993.

Dropkin, Lisa, Hollis A. Hope, and Vikki N. Spruill. *Making American Foundations Relevant: Conversations with 21st Century Leaders in Philanthropy*. Washington, D.C.; FoundationWorks, 2006.

Drucker, Peter F. *The Practice of Management*. New York: Harper and Row, 1954.

Emerson, Jed. "Foundations: Essential and Missing in Action." *Alliance Online Extra* (March 2006). www.allavida.org/alliance/axmar 066.html?pnd (10 March 2006).

"Facts and Figures about Charitable Organizations." Washington, D.C.: Independent Sector, 2006.

Fleishman, Joel L. *The Foundation: A Great American Secret: How Private Wealth Is Changing the World*. New York: PublicAffairs, 2007.

———. "Simply Doing Good or Doing Well: Stewardship, Hubris and Foundation Governance." In *Just Money: A Critique of Contemporary American Philanthropy*, edited by H. Peter Karoff (pp. 101–28). Boston: Philanthropic Initiative, 2004.

Flexner, Abraham. *I Remember: The Autobiography of Abraham Flexner*. New York: Simon and Schuster, 1940.

Frumkin, Peter. "Accountability and Legitimacy in American Foundation Philanthropy." In *The Legitimacy of Philanthropic Foundations: U.S. and European Perspectives*, edited by Kenneth Prewitt, Mattei Dorgan, Steven Heydemann, and Stefan Toepler (pp. 99–122). New York: Russell Sage Foundation, 2006.

———. *Strategic Giving: The Art and Science of Philanthropy*. Chicago: University of Chicago Press, 2006.

Gilbert, Nathan. "Program Officer Team Approach," *GEOlist*. Grantmakers for Effective Organizations. www.geolist@news.geofunders .org (22 November 2006).

"The Good Man." *Time Magazine* (24 September 1956) time-proxy .yaga.com/time/magazine/printout/0,8816,867100,00.html (28 November 2006).

Hager, Mark A., Thomas Pollock, Kennard Wing, and Patrick M. Rooney. "Nonprofit Overhead Cost Project: Facts and Perspectives, Brief No. 3." Indianapolis: Center on Nonprofits and Philanthropy, Urban Institute; Center on Philanthropy, Indiana University, August 2004.

Hegel, Georg Wilhelm Friedrich. *Aesthetik*. www.Britannica.com/eb/article-51139/tragedy#504976.hook (22 October 2006).

Heifetz, Ronald A., John V. Kania, and Mark R. Kramer. "Leading Boldly: Foundations Can Move Past Traditional Approaches to Create Social Change through Imaginative—and Even Controversial—Leadership." *Stanford Social Innovation Review* 3 (Winter 2004): 21–31.

Henley, Beth, Francie La Tour, Sacha Pfeiffer, and Michael Rezendes. "Some Officers of Charities Steer Assets to Selves." *Boston Globe* (9 October 2003).

Jones, Anna Faith. "Doors and Mirrors." In *Just Money: A Critique of Contemporary American Philanthropy*, edited by H. Peter Karoff (pp. 51–62). Boston: Philanthropic Initiative, 2004.

Josephson, Michael. *Ethics in Grantmaking and Grantseeking: Making Philanthropy Better*. Marina Del Rey: Joseph & Edna Josephson Institute of Ethics, 1992.

Karoff, H. Peter. "Saturday Morning." In *Just Money: A Critique of Contemporary American Philanthropy*, edited by H. Peter Karoff (pp. 3–22). Boston: Philanthropic Initiative, 2004.

Kibbe, Barbara D., Fred Setterburg, and Colburn S. Wilbur. *Grantmaking Basics: A Field Guide for Funders*. Washington, D.C.: Council on Foundations, 1999.

King, Max. "Riskier Days Ahead for Stodgy Foundations." *Pittsburgh Post-Gazette*, 7 May 2006. www.post-gazette.com/pg/pt/06127/688156.stm (12 May 2006).

Klein, Kim. *Fundraising for Social Change*. San Francisco: Jossey-Bass, 2001.

Letts, Christine, William Ryan, and Allen Grossman. "Virtuous Capital: What Foundations Can Learn from Venture Capitalists." *Harvard Business Review* (March/April 1997): 36–44.

McDonald, Dwight. *The Ford Foundation: The Men and the Millions: An Unauthorized Biography*. New York: Reynal, 1956.

"New York School of Philanthropy." *Wikipedia*. en.wikipedia.org/wiki/New_York_School_of_Philanthropy (5 March 2007).

Nielsen, Waldemar A. *The Big Foundations.* New York: Columbia University Press, 1972.

———. *The Golden Donors: A New Anatomy of the Great Foundations.* New York: E. P. Dutton, 1985.

"The Nonprofit Biz: Tax-Free Institutions Have Multiplied; Many Simply Aren't Worth the Cost." *Philadelphia Inquirer,* 25 April 1993.

Orosz, Joel J. *The Insider's Guide to Grantmaking: How Foundations Find, Fund and Manage Effective Programs.* San Francisco: Jossey-Bass, 2000.

Pifer, Alan J. "Speaking Out: Reflections on 30 Years of Foundation Work." *Foundation News and Commentary* 38, no. 4 (July/August 1997) www.foundationnews.org/CME/article.cfm?ID=2377 (9 December 2006).

Prager, Dennis J. *Organizing Foundations for Maximum Impact: A Guide for Effective Philanthropy.* Washington, D.C.: Aspen Institute, 2003.

Prewitt, Kenneth. "American Foundations: What Justifies Their Unique Privileges and Powers." In *The Legitimacy of Philanthropic Foundations: U.S. and European Perspectives,* edited by Kenneth Prewitt, Mattei Dorgan, Steven Heydemann, and Stefan Toepler (pp. 27–46). New York: Russell Sage Foundation, 2006.

Proscio, Tony. *Bad Words for Good: How Foundations Garble Their Message and Lose Their Audience.* New York: Edna McConnell Clark Foundation, 2000.

———. *In Other Words: A Plea for Plain Speaking in Foundations.* New York: Edna McConnell Clark Foundation, 2000.

Raymond, Susan. "American Philanthropy and the Twenty-first Century: A Plea for the World of Ideas." *On Philanthropy 2005.* onphilanthropy.com/articles/print.aspx?cid=744 (8 December 2005).

Renz, Loren, Steven Lawrence, and Josefina Attenzai. *Foundation Growth and Giving Estimates.* New York: Foundation Center, 2006.

Schroeder, Steven A. "When Execution Trumps Strategy." In *Just Money: A Critique of Contemporary American Philanthropy,* edited by H. Peter Karoff (pp. 179–202). Boston: Philanthropic Initiative, 2004.

Sherman, Scott. "Target Ford." *The Nation* (5 June, 2006). www.thenation.com/doc/20060605/sherman (11 November 2006).

Sievers, Bruce. "If Pigs Had Wings." *Foundation News and Commentary* 38, no. 6 (November/December 1997): 44–45.

———. "Philanthropy's Blind Spots." In *Just Money: A Critique of Contemporary American Philanthropy*, edited by H. Peter Karoff (pp. 129–50). Boston: Philanthropic Initiative, 2004.

Skloot, Edward. "Slot Machines, Boat Building and the Future of Philanthropy." *Responsive Philanthropy: The NCRP Quarterly* (Spring 2002): 1, 14–16.

Snow, C. P. *The Two Cultures and the Scientific Revolution*. Cambridge: Cambridge University Press, 1959.

Weaver, Warren. *American Foundations: Their History, Structure, Management, and Record*. New York: Harper and Row, 1967.

Wheatley, Steven C. "The 'Natural History' of Philanthropic Management." *Center for the Study of Philanthropy Working Papers*. Indianapolis: Center on Philanthropy of Indiana University, 1989.

Wilhelm, Ian. "Giving Charities a Voice: Organization Offers Foundations an Unvarnished Evaluation." *Chronicle of Philanthropy* 17, 10 November 2005.

———. "Michigan A.G. Investigates Ford Foundation, Seeks Increase in Grants for the State." *Chronicle of Philanthropy* 18, 6 April 2006.

www.case.edu/mandelcenter (12 September 2006).

www.charitynavigator.org (22 October 2006).

www.cof.org (12 September 2006).

www.foundationcenter.org/findfunders/statistics/gm_staff.html (5 March 2007).

www.geofunders.org (9 December 2006).

www.givingforum.org (12 September 2006).

www.grantcraft.org (12 September 2006).

www.grantmakingschool.org (12 September 2006).

www.gvsu.edu/jcp (12 September 2006).

www.philanthropy-iupui.edu/exmu.html (12 September 2006).

www.philanthropy.iupui.edu/phd.html (12 September 2006).

www.smallfoundations.org (12 September 2006).

INDEX

ABOUT THE AUTHOR

Joel J. Orosz is distinguished professor of philanthropic studies and founding director of The Grantmaking School at the Dorothy A. Johnson Center for Philanthropy and Nonprofit Leadership of Grand Valley State University, with campuses in Allendale and Grand Rapids, Michigan. He was formerly the Program director at the W. K. Kellogg Foundation responsible for establishing and developing the Foundation's Philanthropy and Volunteerism programming area. He serves as a trustee of the Guido A. and Elizabeth H. Binda Foundation in Battle Creek as well as the Burton H. and Elizabeth S. Upjohn Charitable Trust in Kalamazoo, and is a member of the advisory committee of the Center for Effective Philanthropy in Cambridge, Massachusetts.

Professor Orosz is a graduate of Kalamazoo College, and earned his M.A. and Ph.D. degrees from Case Western Reserve University in Cleveland, Ohio. Among other works, he is the author of *The Insider's Guide to Grantmaking: How Foundations*

Find, Fund and Manage Effective Programs; Curators and Culture: The Museum Movement in America, 1740–1870; the co-author of *Agile Philanthropy: Understanding Foundation Effectiveness;* and the editor of *For the Benefit of All: A History of Philanthropy in Michigan;* as well as the author of numerous articles, book chapters, and encyclopedia entries on philanthropy, volunteerism, museology, and numismatics.